The Ultimate Challenge

The Ultimate Challenge

Single-handed Round the World

The Story of The BOC Challenge 1982-83

Barry Pickthall

With an introduction by
Robin Knox-Johnston, CBE

Orbis Publishing·London

Half-title: *Crédit Agricole* **in Table Bay after the first leg, from Newport to Cape Town.**

Title-page: Paul Rodgers at the wheel of his Class 1 entry, *Spirit of Pentax.*

Author's acknowledgment

The author gratefully acknowledges the assistance given him by competitors and officials of The BOC Challenge during the preparation of this account of the race.

First published in Great Britain by Orbis Publishing Limited, London, 1983

ISBN 0-85613-560-7

Printed in SPAIN
by Grijelmo, S. A.

Contents

Foreword

We think of the human family as one of great diversity. Some human beings start life with greater advantages than others – physical, psychological, sometimes social, often economic. However, these advantages and disadvantages with which we are born or reared fail to explain the achievements of those very rare individuals who are clearly set apart from the rest of mankind.

These men and women seem determined to create or grasp opportunities for extraordinary challenge. They set standards and goals for themselves that are beyond the comprehension of the rest of us. In conquering these challenges, they drive themselves with persistence, energy, courage and skills which astonish us. We see this in all walks of life: business, sports, and high adventure.

There can surely be few endeavours more demanding of these qualities in an individual than The BOC Challenge single-handed yacht race around the world – an event that proved to be so much more than just a long-distance sail-boat race.

By the spring of 1982, several hundred enquiries about The BOC Challenge had translated into thirty-four firm entries. Half that number crossed the start line in Newport, Rhode Island, on 28 August 1982, and just ten completed the course in the early summer of 1983. They ranged in age from their late twenties to their late fifties. They included a real-estate developer, a chemist, a deep-sea diver, a newspaper editor, a taxi driver, and a refugee from the Eastern bloc. They had little in common except those qualities that turn ordinary men into heroes.

The race itself had its moments of both high drama and comic relief, acts of great seamanship and dramatic rescues in the raging Southern Ocean. The sense of competition between the entrants, that became more intense as the race progressed, was overlaid with an uncanny bond of friendship and camaraderie that can only exist between people who share the traumas of a unique and gruelling experience. This book is their story. At The BOC Group we were proud to know these men and to be involved in their quest to conquer what has become known as *the ultimate challenge* for any individual.

Richard V. Giordano
Chief Executive Officer
The BOC Group

Introduction

Circumnavigating the world in a small boat, single-handed, by the route that takes you south of all the main land masses with the exception of Antarctica is certainly the ultimate in sailing challenges and, arguably, the hardest sporting or adventurous feat yet discovered by man. In no other challenge is a person forced to rely to such extent on his or her own resources, or placed quite so far from any possible assistance in the event of an emergency. In all other sports, when the contestant gets tired, or conditions deteriorate, he can drop out or camp until things improve. When conditions deteriorate at sea, the sailor must stay awake and alert handling the boat for his own preservation. Add to the sheer mental and physical effort to survive the pressure of racing, and the prospect becomes enough to daunt even the stoutest heart.

The BOC Challenge put seventeen maritime adventurers to this ultimate test, and ten successfully came through it. Anyone who has sailed through the Southern Ocean can appreciate their achievement. The winds can blow at Force Twelve or more for days on end, and the body becomes a mass of bruises from being bounced around in the confined space of a small boat's cabin. Perhaps the most frightening aspect of the Southern Ocean is the sheer size of the waves. It has been calculated that one wave in 300,000 can reach a height of 36 m (120 ft). When you look astern, and see a wave approaching this height sweeping towards you, there is little you can do except pray.

It is the constant repetition of difficult conditions which is so wearing on both boat and sailor. In the other great single-handed classic, the OSTAR, the total distance is less than one tenth of a circumnavigation, and the average time for the passage is under thirty days, the record being just short of eighteen days. Each of The BOC Challengers sailed at least two and a half OSTARs on each of the four legs of the race, and they completed the course in times that are the equivalent of a sixteen to twenty-two days Atlantic crossing.

The winner of The BOC Challenge, Philippe Jeantot of France, who led the Class 1 boats from the start, set a new world record for a circumnavigation, and beat the previous record by ten days. His boat had been especially designed for the race and looked very well prepared at the start. As the race developed, it became obvious that only damage to the boat or physical injury to the sailor could stop a clear victory, and fortunately neither occurred. Even in the smaller Class 2, the winner came in after about 200 days, very closely followed by the second and third. Class 2 in fact became a much more interesting race, and the winner, Yukoh Tada of Japan, was beaten in the last leg by Francis Stokes from the USA, who came second in the Class overall.

But The BOC Challenge was not just about running and winning a race, it was about people, and their attempts to achieve their ultimate ambitions. Before the start in Newport the contestants were, understandably, on edge, and there was a very strong competitive feeling in the air. By halfway through the course, the surviving contestants had become a private and very friendly club, aiding each other when help was required. They showed that the shared experience, and the mutual respect for each others' abilities to survive that experience, had in some ways become more important than who was winning. At the finish, the successful Challengers had that quiet air of confidence and self-knowledge about them that comes to those who have looked raging nature in the eye.

There has been one other single-handed around the world race, in 1968 for the *Sunday Times* Golden Globe Trophy, but it was a much less organized affair. The BOC Challenge was set up very differently, although the sponsor did not come onto the scene until fairly late in the day. Dave White's original plan brought in over 400 enquiries, and it was soon obvious that he had hit upon an idea that really appealed to the adventurous spirits in the sailing world. Only one thing was missing, and that was the funds to support such a race, which could nowhere near be covered by race entry fees, and he and Jim Roos set about trying to find a sponsor.

The marriage of the race and The BOC Group as its sponsor is almost a story in itself, and came in the nick of time. The BOC Group is a worldwide organization that has operations in all the countries chosen for the three stops. The idea of connecting these worldwide interests in a way that involved enterprise, adventure and risk, all the requisites of a successful business, appealed to them, and they agreed to sponsor the race in March 1982. It was shortly after this decision that they asked me to act as Chairman of the Race Committee, and I was delighted to accept.

Our Committee was a mixed bunch. For a start the Chairman had never been on a race committee before, and felt like a poacher turned gamekeeper, but this lack of experience was more than made up for by the dedication and ability of the others. Fred Alofsin represented the Rhode Island State Yachting Committee, and marshalled the official support. Peter Hegeman, as Commodore of the Goat Island Yacht Club, brought with him the seemingly endless talent from within his membership to tackle the hundred and one tasks that are piled on to those organizing the start of a major yacht race. These two had fielded the OSTAR and Two-Star which finished in Newport, which is how I first met them, and had plenty of experience of dealing with single-handers. The more regular side of yachting was represented by Robin Wallace from the Ida Lewis Yacht Club in Newport, whose immense experience in helping to organize the America's Cup races was invaluable to us. Jim Roos, the Race Director, had been with the race since the first pint. We co-opted Pete Dunning, the Manager of the Goat Island Marina, because of his experience with single-handed races, and his ability to see straight to the solution of any problem. Dick Kenny, an independent consultant, and Nigel Rowe from The BOC Group, completed the team.

In the usual run of races, the sponsor is mainly concerned with the publicity of the event. In our case the sponsor took a very active part in the race organization as a whole, going so far as to provide technical support for the contestants in each port, and helping with their victualling. However, one of the greatest contributions was to agree to pay the not inconsiderable costs of fitting each of the boats with a satellite tracking system. At our first Committee meeting, we devoted nearly all our time to discussing just how we could improve safety for the competitors and lessen the risks that we knew they would be running. It does not matter how much equipment is fitted to a boat to attract attention if the nearest assistance is over 2000 miles away, as is the case in the Southern Ocean. Competitors would have to help one another. At every race briefing, therefore, we emphasized the importance of regular radio communications, not just with Race Headquarters, but with fellow competitors. Although we expected that there would be dramas, no one could have anticipated the loss, and subsequent rescues, of Tony Lush and Jacques de Roux, which were only made possible because the satellite tracking system on all the boats had an SOS button which could tell us that someone was in trouble, and also tell us, to within a mile or two, exactly where they were. This, combined with excellent communications via the ham amateur radio network, saved these two lives.

The rescue of Jacques de Roux by Richard Broadhead will surely go down in the annals of the sea as one of the great feats of courage and seamanship, and one of my warmest memories of the race is of the French yacht *France 3*, which was in Newport for the America's Cup, sailing over as Richard crossed the finish line to give him three cheers for the rescue of their fellow countryman.

After the race was over, and before everyone went their different ways, we held a wash-up in Newport, attended by the Committee and contestants only. The objective was to see what safety lessons had been learned, and discuss how the race could be improved. It was hard to realize that a quarter of the people who have ever sailed around the world single-handed south of the three continents were in that room. As the meeting began to break up I asked all the contestants if they would do it again, and immediately all but one said yes. Then Dan Byrne looked around at his friends and said: 'What the heck, let's make that unanimous.'

The same week The BOC Group announced that they would be running the BOC Challenge again in 1986.

Robin Knox-Johnston, CBE

Single-handed Sailing:
The Early Years

'Sail alone around the world — they must be mad!'

If the seventeen sailors frantically preparing themselves for the longest yacht race in the world could have received a dollar for every time that remark was made by onlookers down at the Goat Island marina, Newport, Rhode Island, at the end of August 1982, the kitty might have kept everyone in beer for the full 27,000-mile voyage. Yet among those mostly incredulous spectators there must have been many who, deep down, wished they too could just set off to sail the world. Sailing alone through tranquil seas towards the sunset is the ultimate escapist dream for those tied down by careers, marriage or mortgage.

Those sailors gathered at the American port knew differently, however. Each of them had completed a 1000-mile proving trial, most had competed in previous single-handed races across the Atlantic or Pacific and two had circled the globe single-handed already. Each had already faced the very real problems of loneliness. Each knew of the dangers to be overcome before they could join that exclusive club of eighty or so single-handed sailors who have made the circumnavigation already. Each had read the spine-chilling episodes recounting huge seas, icebergs, whales and hurricane force winds, set down by Slocum, Chichester, Rose, Knox-Johnston and Blyth after their round-the-world·voyages. Each knew they too faced the ultimate test of endurance, determination and seamanship — alone.

Though luck would inevitably play its part, each of those sailors also knew before the gun had fired that success or failure would rest largely on their own abilities. The first solo round-the-world race back in 1968 sponsored by the *Sunday Times* in London had only one finisher. Robin Knox-Johnston, a 29-year-old officer in the British Merchant Navy, sailing the 9.88-m (32 ft 5 in) traditional ketch *Suhaili* completed the 30,000-mile circumnavigation non-stop in 313 days. The other eight competitors all dropped out, one committing suicide during the event, another afterwards.

Before this second challenge was to get under way thirteen years later, Knox-Johnston, now chairman of The BOC Challenge race committee, said of this Around Alone challenge: 'We expect casualties, we hope there will be no fatalities. We believe there will be some who drop out. But there can be no chance of triumph without the possibility of tragedy, and no ultimate challenge without ultimate demands.'

What is it that compels a man to throw off the shackles of ordinary life for nine months? Fame is certainly one attraction, but that does not explain the motives of the entrants with little or no chance of winning. 'They are in it for something entirely different,' Knox-Johnston explained. 'They are competing to prove themselves and gain the personal satisfaction of facing a savage ocean and winning through. Many will be frightened near to death, but they will live with that fear and master it alone. They will push themselves past their own personal limits and as a result will get a sense of satisfaction that I can only describe as sheer ecstasy.'

All these sailors faced the nagging worry of being run down as they sailed south across some of the world's busiest shipping lanes in the north Atlantic, and the frustration of lying becalmed in the Doldrums with the belief – real or imagined – that others must be doing better. As they sailed on from Cape Town to Sydney and around Cape Horn to Rio de Janeiro, before starting on the last tactical leg back to Newport, they would be running a gauntlet through the ice-strewn seas of the Roaring Forties and the Screaming Fifties where storms are a threat. There was also the ever-present danger, not from the sea itself, but from the proximity of land and the worry this brings of running aground.

Today's solo sailors do have some aids, however. Satellite navigation equipment can pinpoint a yacht's position to within 200 metres (200 yards) seven or eight times a day. Roller reefing equipment removes much of the labour – and danger – of working on a pitching deck furling headsails. Self-tailing winches simplify sail handling, and self-steering gear – the greatest aid of all when it works – frees the solo sailor from the helm to change sails, make repairs and most important, to get some rest.

The first circumnavigator to sail single-handed had to manage without any of these aids. Joshua Slocum, a naturalized American

The first single-handed circumnavigation of the world, by Joshua Slocum, was relatively leisured. When he arrived at Newport, Rhode Island, on 27 June 1898, he had spent three years, two months and two days on the 46,000-mile journey.

born in Canada set out from Boston, Massachusetts, on 24 April 1895 to sail the seven seas aboard the 11.20-m (36 ft 9 in) gaff-rigged cutter *Spray*. He had no preconceived course, just a yearning for travel and adventure, and made many breaks in his voyage to replenish food stocks, or merely to take a rest from the sea. First he sailed across the Atlantic via the Azores to Gibraltar, before heading south to Pernambuco, Rio de Janeiro and Montevideo in South America. His course then took him through the Straits of Magellan into the Pacific to avoid Cape Horn and then on via Juan Fernandez and Samoa to Australia, where he spent some time ashore. He then sailed north, passing inside the Great Barrier Reef to cross the Indian Ocean via Christmas and Cocos Islands, Rodriguez and Mauritius to Durban, rounding the 'Cape of Storms' over Christmas 1897 bound for the 'Tavern of the Seas', Cape Town.

After a stay that lasted almost three months Slocum sailed north once more, calling at St Helena and later Ascension Island, where he had his yacht officially fumigated to prove he was the only one on board, before crossing his outward track on 9 May 1898. Taking full advantage of the Brazil current, he sailed along the South American coast towards the Caribbean, calling at Grenada and Antigua before braving a tornado to reach Newport, Rhode Island, at 1.00 AM on 27 June 1898, having covered more than 46,000 miles around the world in three years, two months and two days, an average of 100 miles per day, not counting stops.

Spray had been built over the frames of an oyster sloop bearing the same name that had first served on the coast of Delaware almost 100 years before. Slocum had seen the wreck propped up in a field at Fairhaven and set about rebuilding her, adding to her freeboard 457 cm (18 inches) forward, 305 cm (12 inches) amidships and 356 cm (14 inches) to her stern to make her a better deep-water ship. Of labour-saving devices there were none. Sails were hoisted by hand, halyards were rove through simple ship's blocks and sheets were all belayed aft. The windlass and her smallest anchor, together with the carving on the end of the cutwater, came from the original *Spray* and she relied on concrete for ballast, for there was no iron or lead in her keel. There was no self-steering system either but, once set up, this little yacht was so well balanced she could hold a true course for weeks on end – a fact even the ablest seamen of the day found hard to believe. Answering doubters at the time, Slocum wrote in his book *Sailing Alone Around the World*: '... see the run the *Spray* made from Thursday Island to the Cocos Islands, 2,700 miles with no one at the helm in that time save for about one hour, from land to land. No other ship in the history of the world ever performed, under similar circumstances, the feat on so long and continuous a voyage.'

During the voyage Slocum changed *Spray's* rig from sloop to yawl, which reduced the size of her rather heavy mainsail and improved her steering qualities on the wind. She sailed her truest

Spray

Slocum and his cutter, *Spray*, were lost in unknown circumstances in a later voyage from Rhode Island in 1909.

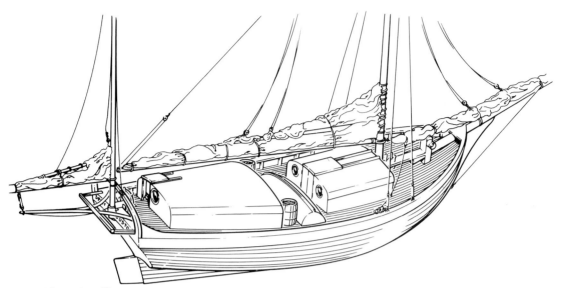

Spray, Slocum's gaff-rigged cutter, measured 11.2 m (36 ft 9 in) and was built over the frames of an oyster sloop that had first served on the coast of Delaware one hundred years before his historic voyage.

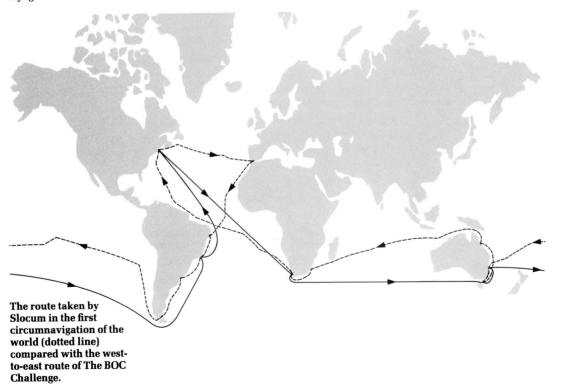

The route taken by Slocum in the first circumnavigation of the world (dotted line) compared with the west-to-east route of The BOC Challenge.

course when the wind was two points off the quarter with her boom set broad and her mizzen furled. Slocum found it never took long to find the right amount of helm required to hold her on her course, and once balanced, the wheel was lashed down. Sailing close-hauled in light winds with all sail set, she required little or no weather helm, but as the wind increased he would turn the wheel up a spoke at a time and re-lash it to keep her on course.

There were some disparaging remarks made about her blunt bows and the wide transom on this shallow draft yacht, but he answered his critics by saying: 'They never crossed the Gulf Stream in a nor'easter, and they do not know what is best in all weathers. For your life, build no fantail overhang on a craft going offshore. As a sailor judges his prospective ship by a "blow of the eye", when he takes interest enough to look her over at all, so I judged the *Spray* and I was not deceived.'

On a later voyage from Rhode Island in 1909, *Spray* and her intrepid owner were lost in unknown circumstances. Did she spring a leak and sink during a storm, a fate Slocum always worried about, or was the ketch run down unseen by a ship at night? It remains a mystery, and though Slocum's loss started an argument that has continued ever since as to whether sailing single-handed is fundamentally unseamanlike or not, it has not stopped an ever-growing number from taking up the challenge.

In fact, the first single-handed trans-ocean race was staged before Slocum's epic voyage by two Americans in craft most of us, even today, would say were not big enough to cross the English Channel, let alone the Atlantic. For William Andrews, who had already crossed the Atlantic in a 5.73-m (19-ft) boat with his brother Asa in 1878, this was to be his second attempt to cross from America to Europe alone and in attempting this feat in a boat a fraction short of 4.57 m (15 ft) back in 1891, he drew a great deal of publicity, both good and bad. It was this press interest that attracted Josiah Lawlor, another American small-boat sailor, to consider the same challenge. Eventually a race was arranged between the two, the course being from Boston to any European port. Andrew's craft, *Mermaid*, had a beam of 1.52 m (5 ft), her 0.61 m (2 ft) freeboard matched her draft, and she was rigged as a gaff cutter. Lawlor's boat, *Sea Serpent*, designed by his naval architect father, apparently matched *Mermaid*'s dimensions exactly, the real difference between the two being that *Sea Serpent* sported a long bowsprit and a spritsail rig.

The two were scheduled to start together on 17 June 1891 but an easterly gale prevented them from setting sail until four days later. Confident that he would make the crossing in fifty days, Andrews set out on a southerly course but capsized on 22 August whilst weathering a storm. Somehow he managed to right her and was fortunate to be rescued the next day by the steamer *Ebruz*, whose crew found him in an exhausted state within 600 miles of Europe, fifty-nine days after setting out from Boston. By this time the race

In 1891 Captain William Andrews, shown here after his subsequent successful Atlantic crossing in *Sapolio*, failed in an attempt to race single-handed from Boston to any European port. However, his challenger, Josiah Lawlor, reached Coverack, Cornwall, safely after forty-five days.

had been lost anyway, for Lawlor, who took a more northerly route, had arrived safely at Coverack, Cornwall, after an eventful forty-five day voyage in which he fell overboard, recovered from two capsizes and fought off an attacking shark.

After describing Lawlor's yacht as a model of architectural skill, the *Western Morning News* in reporting this historic feat went on to tell its readers:

She is provided with two metal air-tight compartments, one forward, one aft, capable of buoying up 270 or 320 kg (600 or 700 lb). The cockpit is 1.83 m (6 ft) long and 0.51 m (20 inches) wide and is covered with a hatch or slide. In rough and rainy weather a rubber apron kept the water out. A drag in the shape of a parachute was used. Captain Lawlor's cooking utensils consisted of an oil stove and a few tin dishes. He carried no stimulants in the shape of strong drink and his larder contained canned meats and beef extracts, chocolate, condensed coffee and milk and plenty of crackers. Forty-five litres (ten gallons) of oil were carried for use in exceptionally rough weather. The voyage was uneventful. For days, however, the boat steered herself in light steady winds and at night after hoisting a good lantern Captain Lawlor could turn in and get some sleep. On 1 July while securing a rope, he fell overboard during moderate weather, but as he always had a rope round his body fastened to some part of the boat he was able to get aboard without any trouble, after a refreshing bath.

On 18 July, while running before a heavy blow, the *Sea Serpent* was thrown on her beam ends and was quickly filled with water. Captain Lawlor, however, promptly jumped upon the keel and was able to right her. As she righted it left him overboard, and the rope around his waist drawing across his hands broke his hold. If it had not been for the rope holding him to the boat he would not have been able to have kept afloat, for he had on three coats and long hip rubber boots, which, when full of water, were a very great weight; and when he succeeded in getting hold of the gunwale he had hard work to pull himself in. The boat was then half full of water; his clothes and everything were wet and disagreeable. He met with a similar mishap while running down to speak with the barque *Finland*, thirty-two km (twenty miles) south west of the Lizard, on 3 August. The *Sea Serpent*, running dead before a nasty sea, gybed over while her Captain was looking for the barque. She went over, and as before, Captain Lawlor had to get out on the keel. It looked as if she would never right; but he finally succeeded by much exertion, and spoke with the barque, whose crew was ready to pick him up.

On the night of 24 July he turned in for the night, there being a light air at the time. He was woken up by the noise made by a shark rubbing against the bottom of the boat. He was turning over to finish his nap, as shark's rubs were a common occurrence, but he was promptly convinced that this shark was trying to capsize or destroy the boat. Looking out, he found a monster doing his best to get a 'square meal' of the *Sea Serpent* and her Captain. The Captain took a patent yacht salute, making a noise like a cannon, lit the quarter-minute fuse and wrapped it in a newspaper and threw it overboard. The shark went for it and just as he turned to seize it the salute exploded. There was a great commotion of the water, and if the shark's head was not blown off he was frightened to death.

Captain William Andrews at Huelva, Spain, in his ballasted folding canoe, *Sapolio*, after the second single-handed trans-Atlantic race, of 1892, in which Josiah Lawlor, the only other competitor, went missing.

After Andrews had been rescued in mid-Atlantic he vowed 'never to undertake such a venture again' but a year later he and Lawlor were to race each other once more, this time from Atlantic City. Lawlor started out eighteen days ahead of his rival in a 4.88-m (16-ft) boat called *Christopher Columbus* and sadly was never seen again, but Andrews, this time aboard a 4.42-m (14 ft 6 in) ballasted folding canoe named *Sapolio*, made it to Portugal in sixty-four days after stopping off at Terceira in the Azores to replace his sea anchor lost during a storm, mend a leak and repair the gooseneck fitting linking boom to mast. Three days later he was in Palor, Spain, where the locals, celebrating the 400th anniversary of the discovery of America, gave him a great welcome. *Sapolio* was later shipped back to the States and put on show at the World's Columbian Exposition in Chicago the following year, where she drew large crowds.

Others might have been satisfied with the fame and fortune he received exhibiting his boat and telling stories of his voyages, but Andrews continued to pit himself against this Atlantic challenge. His fifth attempt in 1898 was abandoned after 27 days, and his sixth a year later he gave up after 21 days. His seventh attempt, this time with his second wife, in a 6.01-m (20-ft) dory, was to be his last. One week out from Atlantic City the two were sighted by a steamer which reported that Mrs Andrews was ill. It was to be the last time they were ever seen. Despite the fate that each met at sea, Andrews and Lawlor set a challenge that has since been taken up by more than 1000 other solo sailors, some in craft as small as 2.75 m (9 ft) long, with one even crossing from Las Palmas to Guadeloupe in a barrel!

Single-handed ocean racing as we know it today did not start until 1960 with the first *Observer* Single-handed Trans-Atlantic Race from Plymouth to New York. It was the brainchild – or brainstorm, as many thought of it at the time – of Lt Col H.G. 'Blondie' Hasler and the redoubtable Francis Chichester. Their cause was the same but their reasons for attempting this 'impossible feat' were very different.

Hasler, a sailor all his life, who led the Cockleshell heroes on a daring raid into St Nazaire, France, to blow up German shipping during the Second World War, was dedicated to improving the design of rigs and steering aids to make life simpler for the short-handed sailor. His testbench was a 7.62-m (25-ft) Folkboat that he had re-rigged with a Chinese lugsail, which he claimed could be set, reefed and unreefed without him ever moving from the cockpit. He had also developed a wind-vane self-steering system and wanted to prove both ideas in a race across to America. Chichester, a London map publisher, liked nothing better than to face a challenge. He had already made a name for himself as a solo pioneer in the air, becoming the second man to fly solo from England to Australia and the first to fly solo across the Tasman Sea – then the longest solo flight in a seaplane on record. A navigator *par excellence*, he was just as keen to take on the Atlantic, saying that if no club would organize a race he would take Hasler on for a private wager of half-a-crown (12½p).

A club did come forward, however – The Royal Western Yacht Club, set at the foot of Plymouth Hoe in England, and the *Observer* agreed to sponsor their event, a partnership that has remained at the forefront of single-handed sailing since. Incredibly there were more than fifty enquiries received by the organizers for that first race in 1965, but once the realities of making such an epic voyage against the prevailing winds and currents dawned, the list shrank to eight firm entries and then five starters.

Four of the competitors in the first Observer single-handed Trans-Atlantic Race (OSTAR), from Plymouth to New York, in 1960. Left to right: Francis Chichester, 'Blondie' Hasler, David Lewis and Val Howells. The fifth competitor was Jean Lacombe.

Francis Chichester, winner of the first OSTAR, accepting a warp on *Gipsy Moth III*.

Opposite: Robin Knox-Johnston, CBE, the first man to sail non-stop single-handed round the world, was the chairman of The BOC Challenge Race Committee.

Chichester's 12.06-m (39 ft 6 in) *Gipsy Moth III* was the largest yacht, but Hasler's 7.62-m (25-ft) *Jester* was matched against three others of similar size. There was the conventionally rigged Folkboat *Eira* entered by the bearded Welshman Val Howells, and the *Cardinal Vertue*, of similar size, sailed by Dr David Lewis. The fifth yacht, *Cap Horn*, of 6.40 m (21 ft), entered by the Frenchman Jean Lacombe started late and finished last. The race was won by Chichester, who crossed the Ambrose light finish line off New York forty days after setting out from Plymouth, some eight days ahead of Hasler, his nearest rival, whose vane self-steering gear had worked so well that he had spent only an hour at the helm during the entire 3,000-mile voyage.

Chichester's achievement captured the public's imagination even though he himself was not too pleased with his time, having expected to finish ten days earlier. 'I hoped to set a time that would be difficult to beat,' he said at a press conference in New York, 'but

every time I tried to point *Gipsy Moth* to New York, the wind blew dead on the nose. It was like trying to reach a doorway with a man in it aiming a hose at you. It was much tougher than I thought.'

Two years later, as if to prove his point, he set out again, this time alone against the clock, and beat his earlier record by a margin of 6 days and 21 hours.

The OSTAR (*Observer Single-handed Trans-Atlantic Race*) has been held every fourth year since and, regarded by all single-handers as the classic test, has brought to fame such names as Eric Tabarly, Alain Colas, Clare Francis and Phil Weld. The number of entrants and size of their yachts swelled with each successive race, reaching a peak in 1976 when the 125 starters from Plymouth Sound faced the severest weather ever experienced during a single-handed race. The race is best remembered for Tabarly's magnificent victory – and its big yachts.

The largest of the 1976 yachts was the 72-m (236-ft) four-masted monolyth *Club Méditerranée* sailed by Frenchman Alain Colas, the winner of the previous race in 1972. She was equipped regardless of cost with every sophistication: satellite navigation equipment, radar and weather facsimile recording machinery, even four television cameras set up on each mast to monitor the set of her sails. Despite all this, the yacht finished only second to Eric Tabarly's *Pen Duick VI*, which at 21.95 m (72 ft) must have been just as much a handful for one man to control, for she was normally sailed by a crew of eighteen.

That race, in which three yachts were involved in collisions and two lives were lost, brought home the very real dangers of sailing single-handed. It had long been conceded that in taking up this personal challenge, all solo sailors broke the first law of the sea – to keep a constant look out and avoid the chance of collision – but so long as they were the ones most open to danger in the event of being run down by a ship, the risk was thought acceptable, at least by those taking part. However, with the emergence of yachts like *Club Méditerranée*, doubts arose about the acceptability of such risks, and after 1976 the Race Committee decided to limit the size of fleet to 110 yachts and to bring in a maximum size limit of 17.07 m (56 ft) overall.

The size limitation caused uproar in France, whose sailors convinced themselves it was all a plot to break their hold on the race, leading them to organize a rival event two years later from St Malo to Guadeloupe in the French West Indies. Called the Route de Rhum, the first event in 1978 was a publicity extravaganza culminating in the most thrilling finish.

After racing 4000 miles through the trade wind belt, no more than a quarter of a mile was all that divided Michel Malinovsky's 21.03-m (69-ft) French monohull *Kriter V* from the winning 11.58-m (38-ft) trimaran *Olympus Photo*, sailed by the Canadian Mike Birch, as the two rounded the northern point of the island on a compulsory

Opposite: The dramatic finish of the 1978 Route de Rhum race, from St Malo to Guadeloupe, helped to popularize long-distance single-handed racing, particularly among the French. After covering 4000 miles, Michael Birch, sailing the small trimaran *Olympus Photo*, snatched victory by a mere 98 seconds from Michel Malinovsky, sailing the monohull *Kriter V* (foreground).

circuit to the finish line off Pointe-à-Pitre. Birch, sailing the smallest yacht in the fleet, one that had been specially extended to meet the minimum size limit set by the organizers, pulled out a useful lead on the light air reach down the western coastline and looked the certain winner until rounding up to beat round the island's southern tip. Inexplicably, Birch took a long port tack out to sea, failing to cover his rival who stayed close inshore playing the shifting wind. By the time Malinovsky had rounded the most easterly headland and cracked off sheets for the final 6-mile close reach to the finish, the Canadian was lying two miles astern. At first it seemed impossible for Birch to recover from that blunder but when at last he too could free sheets, the gap between the two began to narrow quickly. It was like watching a Derby during the final furlong. The crowds lined along the beaches and out in spectator craft started shouting their support. 'Malinovsky ... Vite ... Vite!' 'Viva *Kriter V*!' 'Go Birch go!' they screamed, willing both on as the distance continued to close.

The two finally drew level less than 400 metres (450 yards) from the finish line, Birch taking the gun by a 98-second margin, to make it the closest, most exciting finish of a long-distance race anybody is ever likely to witness. The result had a profound effect on single-handed racing for it did much not only to popularize this solo sport in France, but to vindicate the stand taken by the OSTAR organizers in limiting the size of yachts entering their race.

In order to complete this short account of the growth and acceptance of single-handed sailing, it is necessary to look back to the second OSTAR in 1964 when Chichester finished a creditable second, 2 days 20 hours behind a young French Navy Lieutenant called Eric Tabarly. The Englishman had finally broken his personal 30-day target for the voyage, albeit by only a 3-minute margin, and began the search for a fresh challenge to conquer. First he wrote his book *Along the Clipper Way*, an anthology of stories by seamen and authors describing the pleasure, pain and drama encountered during the testing 28,500-mile voyage under sail from England to Australia and back round Cape Horn. While writing, he was planning to make the same voyage alone and become the fastest to circumnavigate the world in a small yacht. 'The Horn was the big attraction in a voyage round the world,' Chichester wrote later. 'For years it had been in the back of my mind. It not only scared me, frightened me, but I think it would be fair to say terrified me. The accounts of the storms there are quite simply terrifying. The tale of ships lost in that region could never be completed because there have been so many.'

Chichester told himself that anyone who tried to round the Horn in a small yacht must be crazy. According to his researches, of the eight who had attempted it, six had been capsized or pitchpoled before, during or after the passage. 'I hate being frightened,' Chichester wrote, 'but even more, I detest being prevented by fright. At the same time the Horn had a fearsome fascination and it offered

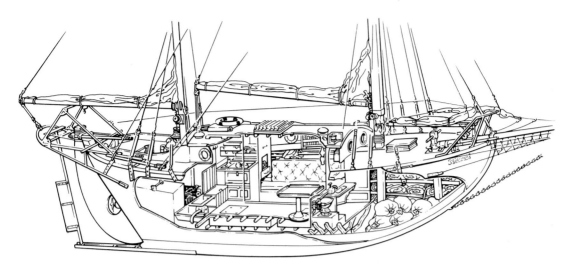

one of the greatest challenges left in the world.'

Setting off from Plymouth at the age of sixty-five on 27 August 1966, aboard *Gipsy Moth IV*, a new 16.18-m (53 ft 1 in) yacht built specially for the voyage, he captured the hearts of millions by sailing non-stop first to Sydney then returning along the Clipper route round Cape Horn to a hero's welcome at Plymouth on 28 May 1967, after spending 227 days at sea alone.

A year later another Englishman, Alec Rose, who had also competed in that 1964 OSTAR, set off from Portsmouth aboard a 10.97-m (36-ft) cruising ketch, *Lively Lady*, to realize a similar personal goal. Though defeated at first by a series of mishaps, he started again on 16 July 1967 to return victorious on 4 July the following year after stopping at Melbourne and New Zealand.

There was now just one major challenge left to conquer – to sail around the world non-stop. At the start of 1968 at least four adventurers had plans to capture this first. John Ridgeway, who had earlier rowed the Atlantic with fellow-paratrooper Chay Blyth, and Commander Bill King were building new yachts paid for with sponsorship money. Robin Knox-Johnston was in the final stages of preparing his existing 9.88-m (32 ft 5 in) ketch *Suhaili*, and Bernard Moitessier from France, who had already circumnavigated the world via Cape Horn, was to put his proven 12.04-m (39 ft 6 in) ketch *Joshua* to a greater test.

As each began finalizing his plans, editors of the *Sunday Times* newspaper in London, impressed by the response they had received from Chichester's regular contributions during his circumnavigation, announced in March 1968 their Golden Globe Trophy for the first person to circumnavigate the world non-stop single-handed, together with two £5,000 prizes – for the first to complete the course and for the fastest time.

In the end nine competitors set out to chase Knox-Johnston, who sailed from Falmouth on 14 June 1968, but like the fable of the

A cutaway drawing of Robin Knox-Johnston's 13.41-m (44-ft) ketch *Suhaili*, in which he became the first person to circumnavigate the world non-stop.

Robin Knox-Johnston
arriving off Falmouth in
April 1969 after his non-
stop port-to-port voyage
round the world.

Opposite: Francis
Chichester's *Gipsy Moth
IV* rounding Cape Horn
on 20 March 1967.

tortoise and hare, it was the slowest boat that finally won. Ridgeway
and Chay Blyth, who also took up the challenge after helping his
former trans-Atlantic rowing partner with his preparations, both
retired in South Africa, King was dismasted during a capsize, the
Italian Carozzo and Frenchman Fougeron both withdrew. Nigel
Tetley's trimaran *Victress* broke up after rounding Cape Horn and
crossing his outward track and Donald Crowhurst committed suicide at sea after pretending to the world for most of the voyage that
he had sailed the course, while all the time remaining in the relative
safety of the south Atlantic. Knox-Johnston's only real challenger,
Moitessier, rounded Cape Horn and looked set to win in the contest
with the Englishman, but decided to sail straight on to pass the Cape
of Good Hope a second time 'to save my soul', ending up dropping
anchor off the Pacific island of Tahiti after 307 days at sea.

Three hundred and thirteen days after setting out, Robin Knox-
Johnston and his battered, rust-streaked *Suhaili*, paintwork peeling,
self-steering gear gone, returned to Falmouth and a fantastic reception on 22 April 1969 to become the first to circumnavigate the world
port-to-port single-handed. The Englishman had faced and beaten
the ultimate trial, and for others the challenge that now remained
was to beat Knox-Johnston's time.

A New Challenge:
The Competitors and Their Yachts

The true genesis of The BOC Challenge is somewhat difficult to trace. Many were involved, and most tell different stories. It would seem that, quite independently, several single-handers in the late 1970s nurtured dreams of competing in a round-the-world race. It was plain that this would represent the ultimate challenge for all of them. For all but one of them, American David White, the dream remained a topic for discussion. White was more persistent, however, and set about trying to get such a race organized.

The idea, like so many good ideas, was given fresh impetus in a bar – a bar in Newport, Rhode Island. The discussion was at the Marina Pub on Goat Island, a traditional watering hole for solo sailors from past OSTAR and Bermuda races. Dave White was there, along with a clutch of other single-handers, and the Goat Island property manager, Jim Roos. White declared that: 'If a single-handed race round the world ever came about, I would certainly build a new boat for it.' And later when the others realized he was serious, Roos undertook to help organize it.

As Goat Island had always been heavily involved in short-handed racing, Newport made a natural start and finish point; but what about the rest of the course? Roos decided to test the water by first writing to the yacht clubs at Cape Town and Mar del Plata in Argentina, who were to host the fully crewed yachts in the 1981 Whitbread round-the-world race. He also threw the idea at the Commodore of the Royal Tasmanian Yacht Club when he was passing through, and when a favourable response was received from all three, the race began to take shape – and so did White's yacht.

Roos and White decided to base their race on the OSTAR, setting a maximum size limit of 17.07 m (56 ft) and include a Class 2 category for smaller yachts ranging between 9.75 and 13.41 m (32 and 44 ft). There was to be no handicapping – the first yacht across the line in each class would be the winner. The only real departure from the OSTAR was to be a rule banning multihulls because of the question mark that still exists over their seaworthiness.

Details of the race were sent to every likely competitor as well as the news media world wide, and the response was almost overwhelming. Both men were quick to appreciate the enormous promotional potential their challenge offered. If the *Observer* and *Sunday Times* newspapers as well as Whitbread, the brewery group, had managed to get a tangible return from the races they sponsored, it didn't take much imagination to realize what a race starting and finishing in US waters might do for a switched-on American conglomerate. To help things along, Roos arranged legal shelter against liability or property loss through a Rhode Island law that protects companies sponsoring events, together with tax-exempt status from the Internal Revenue Service allowing corporations to write off donations as a legitimate business expense. However, they could not anticipate the recession, and when they received little more than polite replies to dozens of presentations, the gilt began to fade. The race would still be on, but not on anything like the scale they had originally hoped.

Left: David White, of the United States, originator of this second single-handed round-the-world race, at the helm of his yacht, *Gladiator*, during early trials.

If hearts were low in Newport, then they were at an even worse ebb in London, where a young adventurer by the name of Richard Broadhead, showing equal determination to compete in the race, was getting the same negative response from more than 800 letters sent out asking for personal sponsorship. His plush and informative brochure ran to thirty-eight pages and he was confident of winning, but despite getting a foot in the door on more than 300 occasions, the answer was always the same.

Above: The British adventurer Richard Broadhead, whose initial approach to BOC for personal support led this multi-national company to sponsor the race.

Then came a chink of light. Executives of one multi-national firm looking for worldwide exposure showed a real interest, even though they had not previously heard of the race. A week or so later, Roos received two telephone calls. The first was little more than a request from an individual in London asking for information. It drew no more than a standard response. The second, however, this time from The BOC Group (a UK-based worldwide company specializing in industrial gases, health care, carbon and welding products) asking whether the race itself was sponsored, made him sit up. The race was not sponsored, of course, and The BOC Group's executives soon made the decision to sponsor the event rather than the man.

Nigel Rowe, Chief Executive, Corporate Communications, at The BOC Group, takes up the story:

We heard about this race through Richard at about the same time we were scratching our heads for an unconventional idea to promote The BOC Group name in our major markets outside Britain. They happen to be America, South Africa and Australia, and we have a Latin American Division too. We liked the concept of this race. And we liked the idea of being associated with the qualities that it epitomizes – courage, determination, stamina, and the ability to distinguish between a gamble and a calculated risk. These are all qualities that, in other forms, are at the heart of good business management. We also felt we could add something to the project beyond money for prizes, promotion and organization.

The Czech sailor Richard Konkolski with his son being greeted by the race chairman, Robin Knox-Johnston, on their arrival in Newport after defecting from the East in order to compete in The BOC Challenge.

In the end, The BOC Group took over all the promotional work and much of the management of the race in each of the stop-overs, helped to appoint local race committees in each port, and brought in Robin Knox-Johnston as Chairman of a reconstituted overall Race Committee. In fact, yachting and Knox-Johnston were not entirely unknown to The BOC Group. In 1974, it sponsored Knox-Johnston's successful campaign to win the Round Britain Race in a 21.34-m (70-ft) catamaran.

The BOC Challenge – Around Alone became a natural choice in naming the race, and the company's sponsorship was announced at a series of press conferences in London, New York, Cape Town and Sydney, around the middle of March 1982, five months before the start of the race. The attendant publicity BOC's involvement attracted to this new race helped others to find greater financial assistance from industry which, now that the race had official backing, began to show a willingness to sponsor individuals.

The Hobart and Mar del Plata stop-overs were changed to Sydney and Rio de Janeiro because of their better international standing, and Robin Knox-Johnston's experience was to prove invaluable, not least because most found it hard to argue when a decision of his went against them, Knox-Johnston being in the position of one who had done it all before. One of his first decisions was to bring the start date forward a month from the end of

September, which did not please everyone. In his judgment, though, the smaller yachts – and there were far more entered than the originators had envisaged – might not have got round the Horn before the summer 'weather window' closed on them and this notorious outpost was beset once more by autumn storms.

By this time (March 1982), Jim Roos had received more than 450 enquiries from thirty countries and the entry list looked like being thirty-four strong, representing eleven nations.

Among them were well-known single-handed yachtsmen like South Africa's Bertie Reed, Desmond Hampton from Britain, the Americans Dave White, Tony Lush and Francis Stokes, together with Guy Bernardin and Jacques de Roux from France, all of whom had cut their teeth in past OSTAR events. Also numbered in the list with apparently just as good a chance of success were a taxi driver from Tokyo, two restaurant owners and a French chef, a 60-year-old grandmother from Sydney, a Bulgarian tugboat captain, an Antarctic dog-sled driver, a plantation worker, an oil-rig diver and two journalists, one a woman. For three other contestants, this was to be their second bite at the cherry, Paul Rodgers from Britain having returned only two months before from a solo attempt to circumnavigate the globe non-stop twice!

Each competitor had his own reason for undertaking the challenge. Some were using the race to fulfil life-long ambitions to round the world and Cape Horn in particular. Others hoped it would help them to escape from the dullness of life and its routine. Some saw it as pure adventure. Only a few had any real hope of winning.

America headed the list with six entrants. There was Dave White, of course, the race founder. This giant 37-year-old from San Francisco looked as if he could go ten rounds with anyone, and his large, weather-beaten, lacerated hands seemed strangely at odds with the delicate world of electronics in which he had worked during the previous nine years. A veteran of past OSTAR, Two-Star and a trans-Pac race in which he had spent fifty-two days at sea, he had been happy enough just to finish those events. 'I thought I was doing well just because I did them, but this time I'm out to win,' he told me emphatically in Newport just before the start.

Once he and Roos had got a positive response for their race, White decided that if he was going to build a boat, he might just as well build a winner. He commissioned the experienced designer Alan Gurney to draw up a 17.07-m (56-ft) cutter similar in lines to his other famous designs, *Windward Passage* and *Great Britain II*, then set about to build it himself. The work took nearly two years to complete and the red-hulled yacht was ready for her first trials and publicity photographs on 16 March 1982, the date BOC announced their involvement. Two days later he set out with two friends heading for warmer weather in the south to give the yacht her first real trial – a test that turned into near disaster.

'It was snowing the day we left,' White recalled, 'but the weather was fairly decent. A couple of days out we were going to weather nicely with about 30 knots of breeze across the deck, two reefs in the main and the No. 3 genoa set, when all of a sudden the keel started coming off. For three days we had to pump like mad just to stop the yacht from sinking before getting her to a boat yard I knew in North Carolina. Our self-steering also broke so we had to divide the duties up between the three of us, one steering, another pumping, while the third slept. It wasn't a great deal of fun.'

It took White three months to make good the damage and strengthen the integral framing, time that would have been much better spent continuing the search for a sponsor and getting to know his boat. Then, after relaunching the yacht in June, two months before the start, he found to his dismay that the sails, which had been donated by a friend in the canvas business keen to move into sailmaking, were nowhere near strong enough. 'They just fell apart,' White told me in obvious disgust. 'Here I had a guy who was supposedly making sails to go around the world, and he was making them from tissue paper. I reckon he must have been paid off by the competition,' he joked.

Those delays were to prove crucial for by the time he completed his 1000-mile qualifier, which showed up another 101 jobs to be done, White had run out of time. Asked on the eve of the start how he saw his chances, he said: 'I'm under-financed, and that always hurts. If you read Phil Weld's book, he says it takes three things to win: Preparation, Perseverance – and Pocket. I have only one of those. The boat is very easy to sail – and she's fast. But I'm not sure about her construction. The first leg is going to tell a lot. On the first leg I will find out how my boat goes and if she is structurally up to it.' Unfortunately, those words were to prove quite prophetic.

Tony Lush, another of the Americans, was confident he had a strong enough yacht for the challenge. He was, after all, chief of laboratory testing at Hunter Marine in Alachua, Florida, and had overseen the construction of his Hunter 54 cat-rigged ketch which he had built specially for the race. Lush, a short, thickset man with laughing eyes and sense of humour to match, had been one of the tortoises in the 1976 OSTAR, having taken 61½ days to cross the Atlantic in his small monohull, *One Hand Clapping*, but that did nothing to douse his enthusiasm for single-handed sailing. He's an innovator at heart and both his yachts displayed that thinking. The 16.46-m (54-ft) *Lady Pepperell*, named after his sponsor, Westpoint Pepperell, an American textile firm, sported a revolutionary, revolving unstayed rig whose sails could be reefed from the cockpit by pulling on two continuous rope belts to turn the masts and wrap the sails up around them. Here was another Blondie Hasler doing his bit to develop an easily handled rig, but unlike Hasler and his Chinese lugsail, Lush's ideas were left untried in heavy weather before he set out on this race. His 1000-mile qualifying cruise from Florida to the start, the yacht's only real test before the race, was sailed in almost

The American competitor Tony Lush working on one of the radical revolving unstayed masts on his catrigged ketch, *Lady Pepperell.*

dead calm and Lush had to make full use of the Gulf Stream to push him up to Newport. 'I averaged 4 knots just from the current and played it for all it was worth,' the 33-year-old sailor said on arrival. 'I had a blow the last night, but then I didn't want to take any risks because the lee shore was less than forty miles away.' He felt that the two original glassfibre masts were too heavy and made arrangements to have lighter carbon fibre replacements shipped to Cape Town, the first stop-over, to be stepped before he hit the heavy weather of the Southern Ocean. Others, visualizing the conditions down in those southern latitudes, wondered more about the low freeboard and very exposed cockpit of this cruising design, and questioned whether the yacht was really suited to sailing round the world. Lush had no time for such doubts however, for, like White, he and his band of dockside conscripts spent every daylight hour frantically finishing the job of fitting *Lady Pepperell* out in time for the start.

To most minds the dark horse at the start of the race was 30-year-old Philippe Jeantot, an oil-rig diver from Concarneau in France. He had not raced single-handed before but had managed to find time to cover more than 25,000 miles sailing alone just for the fun of it, and now he had a purpose-built, maxi-sized cutter designed by Guy Ribadeau Dumas. This quiet, unassuming Frenchman had spent the last five years diving in the North Sea, Gulf of Mexico, and off the coasts of Argentina and South Africa in search of oil, and in 1977 had set a world record with five others for the deepest dive – 500 metres (1,640 ft).

Divers are by nature perfectionists, for their life depends on it, and it was this quality more than anything else that seemed to put Jeantot's challenge ahead of the rest. When first hearing of the race, he was already planning to make the voyage anyway in his own 13.11-m (43-ft) steel boat, so the decision to enter was a simple one. He realized that his original yacht would be too heavy to be competitive, so immediately set about looking for a sponsor to help defray the cost of building a new design. In France solo racing has become a national sport with hundreds emulating the great Tabarly, so the attendant commercialism required to pay for these feats has become an accepted part of this sport. It was not surprising therefore that Jeantot not only found a sponsor, but attracted more support than any other competitor. Within five months of starting the search, he secured an 800,000-franc donation from the French co-operative

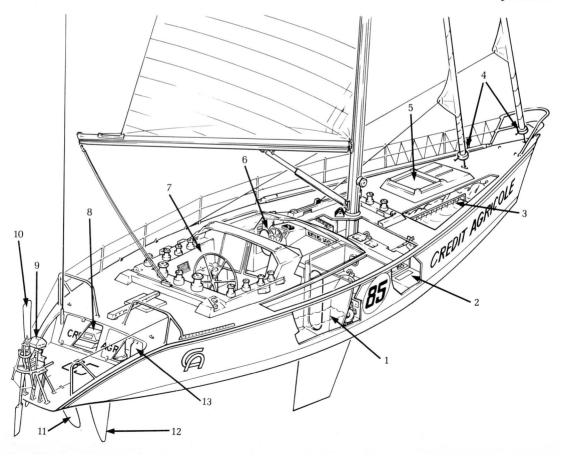

bank Crédit Agricole. Time seemed to be the only thing against him, for the 17.07-m (56-ft) light displacement alloy craft was not completed until 2 months before the start, and five friends had to work round the clock to get her ready in time for the race after making a 20-day Atlantic crossing from France.

Though Spartan below decks, a great deal of thought obviously went into this lightweight design. Instances of this were the interconnected ballast tanks set on either side of the hull to keep the yacht on a more even keel. Once the weather tank had been filled with 1500 litres (330 gallons) of sea water at the start of the voyage, a stopcock connecting the two tanks was opened to allow the water to flow from weather to leeward tank just before the yacht was tacked. This transfer took up to five minutes to complete and increased heel dramatically, particularly in heavy weather, but Jeantot always insisted that the 5000 kg (5 tons) of ballast in *Crédit Agricole*'s keel provided a healthy margin. Though unique to the BOC fleet, this idea was first devised several years before by Eric Tabarly, who had similar tanks in his flat, wide, monohull *Pen Duick V*, the winning boat of the first single-handed trans-Pacific race in 1969.

The French competitor Philippe Jeantot showing one of the two daggerboards that slotted through the stern sections of *Crédit Agricole*. They were used in strong conditions to help keep the yacht on a straight course.

One idea incorporated into *Crédit Agricole* that was original, however, was that of two daggerboards slotting through the stern sections on either side of the centreline. These small foils canting out at an angle close to 30° were designed to act like the fins of a sailboard (which first gave Jeantot the idea) to keep the yacht on a straight course when the going got rough in the Southern Ocean. They were to prove very successful, for the more the yacht rolled, the more upright and thus more effective the leeward fin became, keeping the boat running true when it might otherwise have broached, and taking much of the pressure off the hard pressed self-steering gear. Cutter-rigged, *Crédit Agricole*'s 150 m² (180 yd²) sail plan could be reefed without need for Jeantot to step out of the cockpit. Headsails were furled on hefty French-made Proengin roller reefing gear which, unlike the gear on other yachts, withstood the full 27,000-mile voyage without giving trouble, while the halyard and slab reefing lines attached to the mainsail all led back to self-tailing winches in the cockpit.

The all-important electricity to power radio, sat/nav and weather fax equipment was generated by four large Motorola solar panels mounted on the coachroof which Jeantot jumped and walked on without concern, each panel producing 2½ amps per hour whenever the sun shone. On cloudy days the Frenchman relied on a water-driven Wattas generator which, looking very much like a small auxiliary outboard, clipped over the stern to produce 15 amps per hour when the yacht was sailing at 7 knots or more.

Below decks, the yacht had an effective wheel house from where Jeantot intended to steer sitting on a Renault car seat when crossing the freezing wastes of the Southern Ocean. Though cramped, the bridge deck was completely self-contained and in the event of damage to the hull, could be sealed off from the forward sections by a watertight door. Sails were stowed forward and brought out through a small deck hatch which had rollers set around its periphery to aid this single-handed task – an idea Jeantot borrowed from the Dutch yacht *Flyer*, which won the 1981/2 Whitbread round the world race.

During that last week before the start, Jeantot and his friends worked all hours to get *Crédit Agricole* ready. It was a race against time in other ways too, for the Frenchman's log, proving his 1000-mile solo trial made in the Mediterranean the previous spring, appeared to have been lost in the post, and without sight of it, the Race Committee insisted he could have only provisional status in the race. Might all these last-minute preparations be wasted? Jeantot could only ask friends back in France to send a copy – and take trust in the post that the parcel would arrive in Newport before he reached Cape Town!

All sheets and control lines on *Crédit Agricole* were led back to self-tailing winches around the cockpit to save the skipper, Philippe Jeantot, from having to go out on deck when reefing or adjusting the sails.

One man with no such worries was Bertie 'Biltong' Reed, one of South Africa's best-known sailors, who arrived in Newport eight days before the start, fresh from breaking the monohull record in the Round Britain race with his new Lavranos-designed *Voortrekker II*. This yacht had been commissioned specifically for the 1984 OSTAR when yachts up to 18.28 m (60 ft) will be allowed to enter. Unfortunately, this change of heart in England, which increased the maximum size limit, had been made too late for the Around Alone organizers to change their size limit from 17.07 m (56 ft), so Reed was forced to turn to his original *Voortrekker*, in which he had competed in the 1980 OSTAR. This was the yacht that Bruce Dalling had piloted to second place in the 1968 OSTAR, and despite her age, she was well-proven enough for many to put their money on her.

A 38-year-old instructor at an Armed Forces sailing Academy in Simonstown, sailing has always been Reed's life. His qualifier had been the 1980 OSTAR, where he finished eighteenth after losing time lying hove-to in mid-Atlantic, shoring up the side of the yacht with a jockey pole and the seat from his bosun's chair after the hull had been damaged when crashing down over a wave.

A father of four, the craggy-faced, deep-tanned, blue-water sailor Reed spends more and more time at sea each year, though he conceded before the start that he does sometimes question his motives – like the time he was tossed overboard during a violent storm off Port Elizabeth in 1979. 'The boat was over 160° and I was thrown through the guard rail,' he said. 'I had only a jib sheet to hold on to until the boat came up again. I thought – I really thought – what am I trying to do; but then later I didn't think about it any more.'

'I think the most difficult thing about this race is learning how to pace yourself,' he said of this BOC Challenge before the start in Newport. 'You have to make the right decisions. If you make the wrong ones, you can lose days – and it won't be so easy to keep that up day after day.'

The big advantage Reed had over many of the others was that he knew his yacht well. He knew how hard he could drive her and he was one of the best prepared. *Altech Voortrekker*, as she was to be known in this race in recognition of the sponsorship received from a communications company in South Africa, may have been giving away a 2.13-m (7-ft) advantage to the newer maxis in this race, but the others knew that when the going got tough, it was tough men like Reed that got going.

Another tough man of the sea was the Australian Neville Gosson who, having sailed single-handed from his home port of Sydney via the Panama Canal, making the 11,000-mile voyage in 79 days, had covered almost half the race distance already. A keen sailor for 30 years, this was the first solo voyage for this 55-year-old Aussie, and though he took a short cut through the Panama Canal instead of rounding Cape Horn, it proved quite a baptism. First he hit a whale. 'It was like hitting a reef at 10 knots,' he told us later. 'It was a humpback. It bumped me twice, then I saw it surfing about 200 m (200 yds) behind. It was looking at me almost quizzically – and all I could do was to stare back.' He also suffered two knockdowns and several sails were blown to shreds. On one occasion the boat was slammed by a 180° shift so violent that the spinnaker wrapped around the rigging, forcing him to run off for 20 miles before he could unravel it.

Gosson's 16.15-m (53-ft) sloop, *Leda Pier One*, named after his sponsor, who also played host to all the yachts that arrived in Sydney, had been custom-built for him back in 1974 and looked one of the sturdiest in the fleet. Before the start he had a laid-back air about him, seemingly unworried by the trivia of life. When his sponsor rang race control after his arrival in Newport, asking how his sails were and whether he needed anything, this loner didn't feel it necessary to walk back up the dock to take the call. 'Just tell 'em they're all in shreds,' he said, shrugging his shoulders without a care. But it was equally obvious that he was not about to let the Challenge or age defeat him though, and said before the gun fired that having sailed uphill to get to the start, he looked at the BOC race as much less of a challenge. It didn't turn out that way, of course!

Another Corinthian in this race hoping to win overall was Desmond Hampton. Quiet, stiff-upper-lipped, his deep penetrating eyes and clear facial resemblance to Lord Lucan, whose much publicized 'wanted' posters were undoubtedly filed at every port of call in this BOC race, made him appear the typical Englishman to foreigners. In fact he has often been mistaken for Britain's missing Earl, which prompted him to get a tee-shirt printed specially denying the fact.

Taking a nine-month sabbatical from his job as a partner in the London-based estate management firm Cluttons, 'as a reward for twenty years with the firm', he chartered *Gipsy Moth V*, the last in a line of yachts owned by Sir Francis Chichester. This famous Robert Clark design needed 38 cm (15 inches) cut from her stern to meet the maximum size limit. She may have been ten years out of date and lacking the sophisticated electronics that others in this race relied on, but she was designed for single-handed sailing, was well proven – and fast. She was also ready to go a full week before the start of the race.

Hampton, a 41-year-old surveyor, was first introduced to the sea at the age of eighteen by a former employer and it was on one of those 'gastronomic cruises' that he met his wife Kitty, who has since made an equal name for herself in short-handed racing circles. They bought their first boat in 1974 to continue cruising, but a growing family – they have two daughters – eventually called for a bigger craft. *Wild Rival* was their choice, a name made famous by its designer, Peter Brett, in earlier short-handed races. After buying the boat, Hampton then found he had little option but to race it as well. 'Once Brett had his sticky hand on my cheque, he then waved a

Desmond Hampton, skipper of the British Class 1 yacht *Gipsy Moth V*.

bottle of champagne in the other and said: "Well, you might as well know, she is entered for the next Round Britain race, so you had better get on with it." ... And that's how I started racing.'

'I shared the helm with Kitty in that 1978 event and had a wonderful battle with an identical boat skippered by Bob Lush,' he recalled in Newport. 'There was never more than half an hour dividing us all the way and we just won.' That experience was enough to whet both their appetites, for while Hampton went on to compete in the next OSTAR and Parmelia races before taking on this BOC Challenge, his wife went off 'to do her own thing,' including the 1982 Round Britain race. Looking around at the lightweight fliers moored alongside him at Newport Hampton said: 'One never wishes others to fall apart, but if they do, I must be in with a good chance,' adding with obvious enthusiasm: 'It's the first time I have been in a race and had even an outside chance.'

Another equally keen to get going was 29-year-old fellow Briton Richard Broadhead. After failing to gain BOC as a sponsor, he was

The British competitor Richard Broadhead sailing the 15.65-m (52-ft) *Perseverance of Medina*.

now resigned to doing the best he could with the limited resources he had available. 'With a sponsor I might have been able to win this race. Without one, I will be happy to finish in the first five,' he told me on the eve of the start. He was to do much better than that. An adventurer at heart, this Old Harrovian worked on cargo boats in the Caribbean immediately after leaving school at sixteen before spending twelve months working his way round Australia, first as a jackaroo in the Northern Territory, then as a builder's labourer in Darwin, before becoming a mining surveyor in the west. He later spent two years studying farm management as a prelude to working the family estate, but gave all this up to crew on a trawler fishing the English Channel. In 1975 he set out to travel through South America, spending the next three years working on a rubber plantation and cattle ranch in Bolivia before making a 3500-mile journey by canoe along the Amazon River.

Paul Rodgers, the British yachtsman who had attempted to become the first to sail around the world twice non-stop before taking up The BOC Challenge.

Sailing, however, was his first love, and returning to England in 1979, Broadhead bought a 13.11-m (43-ft) Nicholson-built yacht and promptly set off on a solo voyage to Rio de Janeiro and back. A year later he set sail again in preparation for The BOC Challenge on a solo voyage to Antigua and it was on his return that he first faced death in the eye.

'Several thousand miles from land, I developed the most excruciating stomach pains and without a radio to call for advice could only diagnose it as an appendix,' he told me. 'The pain knocked me out completely and I just lay there in my bunk for several days waiting for my stomach to turn blue and the end.'

In fact it was a hernia and he was treated in hospital once he finally managed to make port. 'After that experience, I think I'm ready for anything the Southern Ocean can throw at me, and I certainly won't be troubled by an appendix – I've now had that taken out as a precaution,' he laughed.

There may have been no doubts about his health, but there were some over his choice of boat. The 15.65-m (52-ft) long *Perseverance of Medina* had been built back in 1973 with no expense spared for ex-newspaper publisher Sir Max Aitken as a British Admiral's Cup contender. She was not a success, however, proving so uncontrollable that she was re-christened 'Perspiration' by racing crews in the Solent. Major changes were made to her rig and keel in an effort to improve these inherent balance problems, but having experienced mostly light head winds on his solo voyage from England to Newport, Broadhead was not to find out if these alterations had been successful until the race had got well under way.

This was not the case with Paul Rodgers, the third Briton in this race, who knew his 16.76-m (55-ft) cigar-shaped schooner *Spirit of Pentax* well. It had after all been home for the past year as he attempted unsuccessfully to become the first man to sail alone round the world twice non-stop. He had eventually been forced to call into Cape Town soon after the start of his second circuit in the Southern

Opposite: Yukoh Tada, the saxophone-playing taxi driver from Japan, who proved to be one of the real 'characters' in this 27,000-mile marathon.

Ocean when the boat sprang a leak and his self-steering failed. It was a remarkable voyage, nonetheless, which he was lucky to survive. On one occasion, he fell from the masthead, breaking two ribs, and lay in the cockpit unable to move for several days. Then on his return voyage to England, he did what all single-handers dread most – fell overboard one night while sailing through the horse latitudes, but miraculously his yacht just turned up into the wind and stopped.

Rodgers was thirty-seven years old, and a former sub-editor with the *Daily Mirror* in London. He had to put his flat on the market and take out a 'massive overdraft' to pay for this latest race. Consequently, his self-steering gear, one of the few new pieces of equipment fitted to his tired, rust-stained yacht, was nick-named Eddie after his bank manager. He had also planned to take a new set of oilskins with him, but US Customs officials insisted on collecting an import fee first, which dug so deep into his meagre reserves that the money he had left was enough to buy food for only 40 days. To make matters worse, US bureaucracy ensured that his clothing did not arrive until after the start.

He had badly needed those oilskins, too, for his yacht was wet, uncomfortable and far from fast upwind. She had undergone little in the way of maintenance since her earlier circumnavigation and many of us thought she was unlikely to make it all the way round. Rodgers seemed quite unperturbed by all this, however, and worried more about the weather. It was not the Roaring Forties that bothered him but the fact that the race led the fleet down through the Atlantic right in the middle of the hurricane season. 'The first three weeks will be the worst part of this race,' he predicted, and for him they certainly were.

Nine were attracted by the challenge of competing in Class 2, for yachts up to 13.41 m (44 ft) overall, which, like Class 1 carried a $25,000 purse for the first home on elapsed time. The most colourful among them was Yukoh Tada, a taxi driver from Tokyo, who sailed his 13.41-m (44-ft) sloop *Koden Okera V* from Aburatsubo to Newport with three friends. *Okera*, meaning 'empty pockets', was in fact the reverse, for the yacht started this race loaded down with every conceivable piece of Japanese electronic wizardry from sonar fish detector to colour radar, fancy radios and sailing instrumentation, together with a clutch of TV cameras and microphones bolted in strategic places to catch every move and comment made by this bright-faced 52-year-old as he worked aboard his floating exhibition.

He might never have made the start had Newport not had a jazz festival. He once saw a film of the event, and so impressed was he with one sequence of a yacht under sail accompanied by a tune played by the American pianist Thelonius Monk that he went back to see it nine more times before buying a boat of his own. That was sixteen years ago but he has kept up those dual interests ever since and carried with him on the voyage an electronic piano and a tenor saxophone to while away the hours at sea. And just in case that didn't

Kiochior Sato, the Zen
Buddhist monk who
travelled from Japan to
bless Yukoh Tada's yacht,
Koden Okera V, before
the start.

fill his spare time, he took the precaution of packing his paint brushes and easel to pursue his interest in abstract art with the idea of holding one-man shows at each of the ports of call!

Slight in stature but not in heart, Tada went to Greenland and the North Pole as part of a Japanese exploration team and sailed across the Pacific single-handed before taking up this challenge. To ensure that he and his boat were prepared both physically and spiritually before the start, he arranged for Kiochior Sato, a Zen Buddhist monk and personal friend, to travel over from Japan three days before he left Newport to bless his boat and pray for all the men in the race with him. 'I couldn't understand a word he said,' New Zealander Richard McBride told me after the rotund monk had finished praying on his yacht, 'but I got a strong sense that it was very sincere.'

The pre-race favourite in this class was the highly experienced 39-year-old Czechoslovakian Richard Konkolski, who used the race to escape to the West with his family. The Czech authorities, who had originally agreed to let him participate, later refused him a permit, so he left home with his wife, son and a close friend, crossed the border into Poland where his 13.41-m (44-ft) sloop *Nike II* was moored, boarded her as if going for a day's sail – and just kept going till he reached England, stopping only in Plymouth to buy provisions before making the trans-Atlantic crossing. All four filed papers seeking political asylum in the United States on arrival at Newport.

A construction engineer, he had competed in more than 40 international races, including the OSTAR classic, and covered more than 95,000 miles at sea, and of these 51,000 miles alone. In 1972 he set out to circumnavigate the globe in a 7.31-m (24-ft) yawl that he had built himself and on his return became a national figure – until leaving in July.

Another with a great deal of experience in this class was the 43-year-old Frenchman Jacques de Roux, sailing the 12.50-m (41-ft) *Skoiern III*. Commander of a diesel-powered submarine based at the French Navy School at Toulon, he had finished thirteenth in the 1979 Two Star trans-Atlantic race and been part of an unsuccessful attempt the following year to set a new trans-Atlantic speed record. A bachelor, De Roux had his yacht built in 1979 for a race from Lorient to Bermuda so he knew his boat, and with thirty years in the French navy, the sea as well.

Another from France who could draw on a great deal of experience was Guy Bernardin, sailing *Ratso II*, at 11.58 m (38 ft) the smallest yacht in the race. In 1979, the 38-year-old set out around the world to better Knox-Johnston's record time only to be forced to retire at Cape Town with equipment failure after 125 days at sea. Nevertheless, he sailed from there back to Falmouth in England without an autopilot, in time to compete in the 1980 OSTAR, the classic race he had set his sights on eight years before. Indeed, the name of his yacht was drawn from it, being OSTAR spelt backwards.

Below: Richard Konkolski's 13.41-m (44-ft) *Nike II* (subsequently renamed *Nike III*), the pre-race favourite to win Class 2.

Right: *Skoiern III*, the 12.50-m (41-ft) yacht skippered by French submariner Jacques de Roux.

Quiet, mild, and with an intense sense of purpose, Bernardin believed that the BOC race was as much psychological as physical. 'For a race such as this, you must clear out all the responsibilities in your life,' he said at the start, noting that he and his wife Mitzi, a former airhostess, had sold their restaurant in Brittany so that he could compete in the race. 'Anything can happen. You must clear your mind from all problems, even from your family. Otherwise, you will feel like you are trailing something behind you. I want to be alone, but I have to concentrate on this. It is necessary if you want to do it properly.'

Though size was more than likely to rule his yacht out of the prize money, Bernardin, who was taking on this challenge simply 'because it was there', was one of the best prepared entries at Newport.

The three Americans and one New Zealander in this class, Dan Byrne, Francis Stokes, Thomas Lindholm and Richard McBride, seemed to have the same feeling for the race. The four all chose traditional designs that would obviously be no match for the greyhounds. They were more interested in a safe passage, hoping perhaps that sturdiness would eventually compensate for speed over the 27,000-mile course. Francis Stokes, 56, had been in the food processing business until 1976, when he sold the firm and moved into yacht brokerage. He first got the bug for blue-water sailing during 1970 in a trans-Atlantic passage from England and, once freed from the day-to-day yoke of business, decided to take a keener interest. He sailed his first OSTAR in 1976 and enjoyed it so much, he had another go in 1980. His choice of yacht for The BOC Challenge was a stock production Fast Passage 39 cruiser eventually named *Mooneshine* late in the day, not because of problems with a sponsor – he had none – but because his wife and five children couldn't agree on anything else. 'I haven't been able to get the family to pull on the same rope,' he said with a sigh.

Why was he entering the race? 'It's just one of those things you'd like to do before you hang it up,' he said at Newport. 'It's something you want to do for yourself. I guess it's just a kind of disease. All of us that have been bitten by this single-handed bug just keep egging each other on.'

Dan Byrne was another late developer. This 53-year-old former newspaper editor from Santa Monica, California, started sailing in a small way back in 1964, spending 300 dollars on a used 4.27-m (14-ft) dinghy that came without instructions. He trailed it to Lake Saguaro, a reservoir east of Phoenix, and taught himself the hard

Francis Stokes, the oldest competitor to take up The BOC Challenge, at the helm of his stock-production 11.89-m (39-ft) cruiser, *Mooneshine*.

way. He found it intoxicating and traded up to bigger and better things, first a Thistle, then a Columbia 22, Columbia 26 and a Cal-34 before finally spotting what he called his 'dream boat', a second-hand Valiant 40 he renamed *Fantasy*. A year later he retired from the newspaper business and entered the 1980 Trans-Pac single-handed race from San Francisco to Kauai, Hawaii. The 2,200-mile course took him eighteen days and he finished fifth in his class. The bug bit, and no sooner had he got home than he sent off for an entry form for the BOC race.

Left, top and bottom: The British competitor Paul Rodgers raced in the slender Class 1 yacht *Spirit of Pentax*, which sailed at an acute and uncomfortable angle of heel whatever the conditions.

Right, top and bottom: Richard Broadhead, another British competitor, was unable to get a sponsor for his entry, the ex-Admiral's Cup contender *Perseverance of Medina.*

Opposite: Guy Bernardin adjusting the wind-vane self-steering system on *Ratso II* at Newport before the start.

Right: Neville Gosson, the sole Australian competitor, skipper of the Class 1 entry *Leda Pier One*.

Below: *Skoiern III*, the sturdy alloy yacht skippered by the Frenchman Jacques de Roux.

Below: Tony Lush, one of the American competitors, frantically preparing a list of last-minute jobs to get his Class 1 entry, *Lady Pepperell*, ready for the race.

The BOC Challenge began appropriately at Newport, the port on the eastern seaboard of the United States where Joshua Slocum completed his circumnavigation of the world. The picture shows the Class 2 favourite, *Nike II* (subsequently renamed *Nike III*), skippered by the Czech Richard Konkolski, leading the way.

Inset: It was at Goat Island Marina, Newport, that boats were moored and underwent their final preparations before the start of the race.

Above: *City of Dunedin's* 'green golly' was Richard McBride's secret weapon whenever the wind freed.

Below: *Gladiator*, a Class 1 maxi built by the race originator, Dave White.

Above: The American Francis Stokes came close to winning Class 2 in *Mooneshine*.

Opposite: Jacques de Roux's *Skoiern III* passing ahead of Tony Lush's *Lady Pepperell*.

It was the doing rather than winning that intrigued him most. 'There's an illusion when sailing alone of being in control of your own destiny,' he said in Newport. 'There's the illusion that you're doing exactly what Columbus, Captain Cook and Magellan did. And there's a tremendous elation. I remember arriving in Hawaii. That made it all worthwhile. You really feel you've accomplished something.'

The worst part of the race, Byrne thought, would be the long separation from his wife, Pat, who ran her own window and door business in Santa Monica and whom he married in 1977. At first she was against him entering. 'She said it was "out of the question". You know, she thought it was too far, too dangerous, too everything.' Later though, she was to be the driving force of his challenge.

Byrne spent a lot of time and thought adapting this stock cruising design, fitting Lexan impact-resistant plastic over the portholes, securing everything below decks that might move. He fitted extra handholds and solar panels on deck to charge his batteries. Two of these were fitted on the coachroof, but another pair, pivoted on brackets, were set precariously above the pushpit around his cockpit, and many of us wondered what would happen to them when the first waved crashed over the boat.

Thomas Lindholm, the third American in this class, was a year older than Byrne and took eighteen months to get to Newport in his 12.50-m (41-ft) *Driftwood*. He and his wife arrived a full month before the off after a voyage that took them from southern California to the Mexican coast, past Central America and through the Panama Canal, around the Florida Coast and north to New England. 'If the start were tomorrow instead of four weeks from now, I could step on the boat right now and go,' he said confidently in Newport.

A former vice officer with the Los Angeles Police Department before joining a law practice in the 1960s, Lindholm took up sailing after flying. 'I used to fly a lot, but then one day I crashed into the sea and decided I'd take up sailing instead. I figured the ocean was calling me,' he said with a smile.

Certainly, he looked as relaxed and ready as anyone during that month spent at Goat Island, but I have to confess to wondering at the

Opposite: The 10-year-old schooner Gipsy Moth V, *originally built for the late Sir Francis Chichester and skippered in The BOC Challenge by Desmond Hampton, had had 38.1 cm (15 in) cut from her original stern.*

Dan Byrne, a retired journalist from California, who entered the cutter Fantasy.

time what he would be doing with the heavy boom crutch and sun awning spread over the cockpit, once *Driftwood* hit stronger winds.

Richard McBride, the last in our line-up for the start on 28 August was, like Broadhead, an adventurer at heart with no fixed roots, though in this race he was to carry the colours of Dunedin, the city on New Zealand's South Island which had contributed most towards this venture. The 38-year-old McBride first tasted adventure at an Outward Bound school in 1961 before spending some time at sea as a fisherman. He later worked for five years as a bulldozer driver and photographer for a mining company before heading a dog sled team on a 13-month Antarctic research expedition in 1972.

He built his steel 12.80-m (42-ft) traditional staysail schooner *City of Dunedin* himself over a period of five years and hoped to use it for youth training after the race. His first solo experience came with his 1000-mile qualifier down into the Roaring Forties, which by all accounts proved to be quite a testing.

In Newport, after having his yacht shipped across to America, McBride said he had no qualms about facing nature head-on or of being alone. 'I'm doing this race because I want to do it,' he said of The BOC Challenge. 'The hardest part will be in maintaining a racing attitude for eight or nine months.' He was right, too!

There were some top names in the single-handed world that were due to start and failed to make the big day. American journalist Judy Lawson ran out of time to plan her challenge, and Ann Gash, a 60-year-old Sydney grandmother, like twelve others, failed to find a sponsor in time. Nothing more was ever heard from Kenichi Horie, the first Japanese to sail round the world alone, who planned to enter with a 17-m (55 ft 9 in) alloy yacht with a pivoting keel that could be shifted to weather. Another, Ben Johnston from England, was forced to abandon his plans after his yacht was stolen soon after completing a qualifying cruise across the Atlantic. His 12.50-m (41-ft) production cruiser *Wibbly Wobbly*, which had taken him two years to complete, was taken from a marina in Fort Lauderdale shortly after he returned to England to make his final preparations, three months before the race was due to start. At the time it was suspected that the yacht had been stolen by Carribbean drug runners. By the time the insurance company had made settlement Johnston had no opportunity to buy a second yacht and complete another 1000 mile qualifier before the 28 August deadline.

One East European who failed to show was the Bulgarian tugboat master Nikolai Djambazov, who had spent the past seven years building his 11-metre (36 ft 1 in) yacht *Tangra* in his back yard. During the last weeks before the start, the word from Bulgaria was that their man was *en route* to Newport but he never showed up. He may never have obtained his exit papers, been caught trying to escape, or run into difficulties while crossing the Atlantic – no one was ever able to find out.

Another cause for concern during the final week was the

Claus Hehner, whose yacht, *Mex II*, arrived on the eve of the start with so many problems to be sorted out that the German skipper was unable to participate in the race.

whereabouts of Claus Hehner's 10.36-m (34-ft) yacht *Mex II*, the smallest entry in the BOC list. Hehner, a 59-year-old architect from West Germany, arrived in town three weeks before the start expecting his son, who was delivering the yacht across the Atlantic, to arrive at any time. Day after day he waited for news but none came and the anxiety began to tell. Finally, when he had almost given up hope, *Mex II* arrived on the eve of the start, having encountered rigging, self-steering and radio problems. For Hehner, who had earlier competed in two trans-Atlantic and Pacific races and who saw The BOC Challenge as his last major event, the disappointment was acute, for the repair work would have set him back a week and forced him to retire.

New Zealander Greg Coles might well have reached the same decision, had he not had the interest of a sponsor to uphold. While most were loading final supplies at Newport, his 13.41-m (44-ft) yacht *Datsun Skyline* was still being shipped across the Atlantic, with her designer Richard Granville and his father on board frantically trying to complete the job of construction. Then, when the sixteen starters were casting off, Coles was just getting into his 1000-mile qualifier on a course out in the Atlantic and back – the first time he had sailed the boat. This futuristic-looking yacht with its revolving wing mast and carbon fibre construction might have looked fast on paper, but whether Coles could make up his eleven-day self-imposed handicap remained to be seen. One thing he did do before setting out from Rhode Island, however, was to make contact with a Newport radio ham by the name of Rob Koziomkowski who agreed to listen out for him – an informal contact that later spread throughout the fleet and proved to be a life saver.

First Leg: Newport to Cape Town

Officials and guests, onboard the 22-m (72 ft 2 in) ketch *Belle van Zuylen* anchored in Rhode Island Sound marking the weather end of the starting line, held their ears in anticipation of the cannon's sharp report as Dick Giordano, Chief Executive of The BOC Group, prepared to pull the lanyard.

'Five ... Four ... Three ... Two ... One' ... BANG!

For most competitors, the fire from that starting gun came not a moment too soon, for it marked the end of months of painstaking preparation. All they wanted now was to get away. It was too late for Dave White to have any further nagging doubts about the construction of his yacht *Gladiator*, Richard McBride could only hope that battery problems shown up at the last moment on his yacht *City of Dunedin* had been solved, and Paul Rodgers was trusting that the wheel steering he had spent the last week servicing on *Spirit of Pentax* would hold up for the first leg at least.

Neville Gosson was one of the few who would have liked a few minutes more. The previous week he had received a distressing telegram urging him to give up the race and return home to save his building company from bankruptcy. He faced an agonizing choice: to continue in the race and lose a lifetime's work, or pull out from a long-held ambition and face equal wrath from his sponsor. The time lost deciding what to do should have been spent finalizing preparations. As a result he was the last to leave the Goat Island dock.

The day of the start, 28 August 1982, brought brilliant sunshine and a southerly force 3 breeze that gave the competing yachts just

Below, left: David White's *Gladiator* has a clear lead as the fleet sets out from Rhode Island Sound.

Below, right: *Leda Pier One*, the Class 1 entry of the Australian Neville Gosson.

enough wind in their sails to escape the disturbance cast out from the hundreds of escorting spectator craft. Indeed, the Sound was so full of well-wishers that Francis Stokes for one never did sight the committee boat. It was a fine send-off, and with applause and good luck messages still ringing in their ears, the competitors headed out to sea. The great adventure had begun.

Not surprisingly, perhaps, some found it took several days to acclimatize themselves to the solitude of the ocean but others had their hands so full solving early problems there was no time for such reflections. Richard McBride, Paul Rodgers and Dan Byrne, for instance, had to spend several hours tweaking the control lines on their wind-vane self-steering gear in an effort to get them to keep their yachts on a steady course, and Byrne, who also had to replace a broken forestay turnbuckle during the first twenty-four hours of the race, suffered the added frustration of dropping his glasses overboard. McBride, given a fright on the second day by Concorde's sonic boom as the British jet flew overhead bound for New York, had another the next day when a whale suddenly appeared less than 45 metres (50 yards) away from his yacht: 'A Biggie', he noted in his log.

For Thomas Lindholm, the 57-year-old Californian sailing *Driftwood*, early unexpected problems overwhelmed him. First the headsail roller reefing gear jammed, then two of his light plywood wind vanes snapped in quick succession in a 40-knot squall during his second night at sea. The final straw came when the auxiliary engine needed to recharge batteries failed to start. 'I found myself asking the question: "If I'm having this many problems two days into the race, what's in store for the next 7000 miles to Cape Town?" and I decided I just couldn't continue,' he said on his return to Newport.

Below: The early problems experienced by Californian Thomas Lindholm on *Driftwood* forced him to retire after only two days.

Bottom: *City of Dunedin* (left), the 10.80-m (42-ft) schooner that was designed and built, over a 5-year period, by the New Zealand competitor Richard McBride (right).

On Wednesday, 1 September, five days out from Newport, the fifteen sailors were greeted with the disturbing news of Hurricane Beryl generating powerful 70-knot winds 1500 miles south-east of them. 'So far she is on a straight course of 285 degrees. If that continues we will pass like trains in the night, but if it curves north, I'll feel like a squirrel in the road not being able to decide which way to jump,' Francis Stokes wrote in his diary. It was the chance of running into a hurricane that had concerned Paul Rodgers so much before the start, but his mind was diverted from thoughts of tempests when *Spirit of Pentax* suddenly hit something underwater. 'Terrible crash – didn't expect the boat to take it, but she did. No sign around, no apparent damage. Very sobering,' he wrote in the log immediately afterwards.

During a more searching inspection later, though, he found to his dismay that the impact had split part of the hull planking as well as a longitudinal stringer on the starboard quarter and concluded from the damage that the yacht must have hit a whale slumbering near the surface.

By the end of the first week at sea, the threat of Hurricane Beryl had subsided and most competitors were showing their frustration at the lack of progress made in the very light winds that prevailed. This was the first yacht race from the United States to Cape Town so the only 'form' skippers could follow were notes on the traditional clipper ship route. This swept on a great circle course across the Atlantic close to the Cape Verde Islands down to the Equator before making a wide sweep passing close to the South American coast down to 35 degrees to avoid the calms of the South Atlantic High. Some decided to chance the shorter rhumb line course south and beat into the teeth of the South-east Trades skirting round the top of the South Atlantic High. Yachts competing in previous Whitbread races from England had done this with success. For them it was the shortest route to Cape Town. However, most chose the traditional clipper course in the hope that the easier reaching conditions south would more than make up for the greater distance they had to sail.

Guy Bernardin, one of the three French competitors.

Initial position reports showed that Richard Konkolski had struck a course furthest east with the idea of benefiting from the following North-east Trades on the far side of the Atlantic which he knew well from past races. Following his track was Guy Bernardin on *Ratso II* but the Frenchman had not better reason than to be taking a different course to the rest of the fleet, a tactic he adhered to for most of the race.

At the other extreme were White, Rodgers and Jeantot – and at the end of that first week they were doing remarkably well, enjoying much better winds to the south of the fleet. The most extreme track was that of *Spirit of Pentax*, which seemed an odd choice for Rodgers as it led him on a long windward track right through the area most notorious at that time of the year for hurricanes – the very phenomena he feared most. Nevertheless it proved to be the course to take, for he was able to keep well up with the two fleet leaders, White and Jeantot. Bertie Reed held fourth place at this time some 400 miles further from Cape Town, with Richard Broadhead aboard *Perseverance of Medina* and Francis Stokes on *Mooneshine*, both within striking distance, 75 miles further astern.

The order was soon to change though, for the next day brought the dramatic news that Dave White was retiring from the race after three large cracks had suddenly appeared across the main bulkhead on his 17.10-m (56-ft) yacht. 'The lions are winning, the lions are winning,' he said over *Gladiator*'s radio to his race partner back at Newport. So disheartened was he that the idea of sailing to Bermuda, 650 miles away, to repair the damage wasn't considered worthwhile and he set a course for Florida, twice that distance, convinced that he could go no further in the race.

At the other end of the fleet, Richard McBride, whose first offshore experience had been when he set out alone on his 1000-mile proving trial into the Roaring Forties the previous year, now knew that his heavy steel yacht *City of Dunedin* was no match against any other in the fleet. It did not worry him unduly; he was using this BOC challenge to meet a personal goal and was going to enjoy it too. 'Of all the hats a singlehanded sailor must wear,' he wrote at the time, 'that of chef seems to fit me least well, so it is of some note

Left: *Ratso II*, Guy Bernardin's entry and, at 11.58 m (38 ft), the smallest yacht in the race.

Right: *Spirit of Pentax*, the 16.76-m (55-ft) 'cigar tube' skippered by one of the three British competitors, Paul Rodgers.

when I make a culinary discovery, no matter how minor. The BOC-presented Quaker cereal is too sweet for my plain taste, but mixed with my own muesli, which was rather bland, the result is excellent! It must be my quarter of French blood no doubt! Now to don my doctor's hat and try to remove a splinter from my foot.'

A week later, it became obvious from the position reports sent back to Race Headquarters at Newport, that the westerly rhumb line course was still paying off best, for Jeantot, now 300 miles ahead of Paul Rodgers, was the nearest to Cape Town. They were followed by Broadhead, Reed, De Roux and Tada, who were all within 50 miles of each other on the great circle route, while Gosson, Lush, Stokes and Bernardin were clustered together a further 50 miles astern. It was a frustrating time, for most sat becalmed for much of the week, teased only by the occasional squall that each hoped was the promised trade winds. Each gust sent them scuttling on deck to reef down before their sails blew out, only to find the breeze disappeared almost as fast as it sprang up, leaving them with the chore of setting more sail again just when they thought themselves shipshape.

Left: The calm conditions, pictured here by Richard McBride on *City of Dunedin*, affected the progress of all the yachts during the first leg of the race, from Newport to Cape Town.

Right: Philippe Jeantot's entry, *Crédit Agricole*, suffered a broken runner, a ruptured freshwater tank and torn sails during the first leg but none of these problems was to stop him from building up a commanding 7-day lead over his nearest rival.

'Light weather still prevails,' Neville Gosson wrote in his log. 'Rain last night and with the 42-g (1½-oz) spinnaker set, made no progress. Had to change to headsail when storms came across and in the process the ring system fouled at the second spreader, forcing me to go up the mast half asleep to clear it at 0400.'

Onboard *Mooneshine*, Francis Stokes lay in his bunk dreaming. 'Very peaceful indeed. The only sound now is a slight hiss of water past the hull and the small click of the log every 1/100th of a mile – $100 \times 28,000 = 2,800,000$ clicks back to Newport,' he mused. But after lying becalmed for 36 hours, 2000 miles out from Newport, the pent-up feelings of frustration eventually got to him too, and he dared the wind to come. 'I launched the dinghy and rowed out with the camera to record my first experience of trade wind sailing,' he wrote in his diary. 'I was nervous as *Mooneshine* seemed to slip away at about 1 knot and my dinghy is a sort of a toy with oars to match. Later I went swimming a couple of times. The water is a wonderful blue and feels cool.'

The situation was little different on *Gipsy Moth V*, one of the yachts taking an extreme route to the east. On 14 September, seventeen days out from Newport, Desmond Hampton wrote: 'Around lunchtime, the wind veers to west and drops, and for a lot of the evening I have been totally becalmed. The question is, is it better to go extremely slowly in the desired direction, or is it better to go marginally less slowly in a direction you don't want to go? The answer is I don't know, but I'm backing the latter! In the list I drop to third; I'm not surprised in view of my lack of wind. Others seem to have slightly more. I gave the positions to Race Headquarters in the evening. I also got *Pentax*'s new position and he has dropped well back. They have no new position for *Crédit Agricole* but he is still ahead of the field, even based on his position of the 12th – all a bit depressing!'

These frustrations only came to an end at the start of the fourth week at sea, when most found the trade winds, though the more dependable breeze did bring further troubles for some. Richard Broadhead reported over the radio to Francis Stokes that the forward hatch on *Perseverance* was leaking badly and that he had to bucket out 90 litres (20 gallons) of water from the bilge. He also said he was having troubles with his engine and asked the American to relay a message to Race Headquarters that if he could not charge his batteries, then he would not be able to transmit.

Position reports at the end of the third week showed *Crédit Agricole* and *Spirit of Pentax* bucking the trade winds in their attempt to strike in from the west. 'Certainly unconventional, but may put them way ahead,' Francis Stokes wrote in his diary. In fact, Jeantot was now closing on the Equator, the South-east Trades having lifted him clear of the Brazilian coast, and after averaging 175 miles a day during the previous week, he had extended his valuable lead to more than 900 miles over Paul Rodgers whose 'windjammer' *Spirit of Pentax* was making heavy going against the headwinds. The rest of the fleet, now spread over a wide area, north-east of the Cape Verde Islands, were led by Bertie Reed and Broadhead with Lush and Hampton trailing a good 200 miles astern.

Philippe Jeantot stayed off the air during the daily informal inter-yacht chat shows on this first leg. 'No one told me the frequencies so I was never able to tune in,' he explained to me in Cape Town, but the 30-year-old Frenchman was not without problems of his own. The first was a ruptured freshwater tank which left him dangerously low. His initial thought was to divert to Recife or Tristan de Cunha to get fresh supplies, which would have lost him the lead *Crédit Agricole* had built up, but he managed to devise a method of distilling sea water in his pressure cooker and supplemented this with water collected in buckets whenever it rained. It still meant he had to ration himself strictly, and he arrived in Cape Town with just a few litres remaining. Potentially more dangerous was the block holding the windward runner that suddenly broke

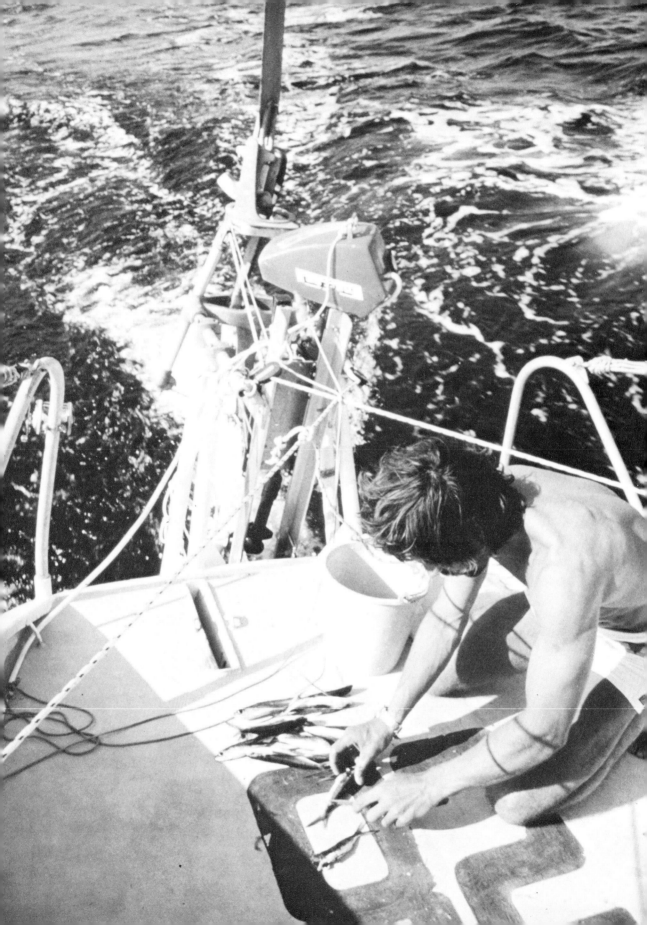

apart as *Crédit Agricole* was beating through the South-east Trades. 'It went with such a bang, I thought the mast was going to break,' he told me later in Cape Town. Luckily for him, the spar proved strong enough to take the sudden strain and, after sighing with relief, he set up a second purchase on the wire.

After a week of refreshing trade wind sailing, the main bulk of the fleet closed in on their next major hurdle – the Doldrums. *Gipsy Moth V* hit this area of humid calm and squalls on 22 September, twenty-five days out from Newport, but there were compensations, as Demond Hampton noted in his diary:

> Entering the Doldrums; tremendous squalls with torrential rain. In one of these I noticed the genoa was torn near the tack. Also, as I was lowering the mizzen, the talaurit splice on the end broke, the halyard pulled through the mast and I had to visit the top to relead it. It had calmed down then but the sea was very rolly. The rest of the afternoon and evening was spent patching the genoa which I managed to do successfully – not terribly beautifully, but quite strong I think. I was quite exhausted by all this activity, particularly after several days of fairly easy sailing in the trades. The squalls provided a splendid opportunity for a fresh-water wash. They also waylaid four flying fish aboard, of reasonable size, which were very good fried with potatoes for supper – which made up for the butter taking off during one of the sudden squalls and plastering itself all around the navigation area!

Guy Bernardin, on a position 300 miles to the north was also being visited by flying fish but Dan Byrne on *Fantasy*, positioned at 13°N, had no time for such luxuries, for he now had his head bowed over the auxiliary, which had seized up while he was transmitting the previous day. He eventually isolated the problem to water in the fuel, which left him with the task of pumping all his stocks through a filter, one pint at a time, to purify it – a job that took him two days to complete.

On *Leda Pier One*, Neville Gosson was in the depths of depression, convinced that he was merely stumbling from one disaster to another:

> Disaster struck just before daylight today (22 September). Violent electrical storm and we were underneath it. Tore headsail but not too bad. However, halyard jammed in the headfoil which meant I could not furl or unfurl my headsail. The trip to the top of the mast was a nightmare but there was no alternative. We spent six hours wallowing around making no progress. Can't afford these stops.

The entry in his log the following day read no better: 'Another dreadful frustrating day. The wind as such went around in circles, never staying in one direction for very long. The constant sail changing left no time for sleep or anything else. Had to deviate around a ship at 2100 hrs in the middle of a rain squall, and blew out

Opposite: One of the delights of sailing in the Trades – fresh flying fish for lunch.

Inside *Crédit Agricole's* wheelhouse, from where Philippe Jeantot steered his yacht in the Southern Ocean. The Danavigate 7000 instrumentation console is positioned to the right of the wheel.

my 14-g (½-oz) spinnaker. Should send him the bill' – he wrote in obvious disgust at the ship's refusal to give way to sail.

Another to experience a similar encounter was Richard Konkolski on *Nike II*, who came across a Yugoslav banana ship one night in mid-Atlantic. As the ship bore down towards him he wondered if his navigation lights had been seen and went below to turn on the spreader and cabin lights as well. The extra illumination made no difference to the ship's course, however, and in the end Konkolski was forced to head up and lie hove-to to avoid a collision.

A second problem taxing Neville Gosson at this time was how to heat up his food. Soon after leaving Newport, he had found that his spare gas bottle, supposedly filled in Australia before he sailed for Newport, was mysteriously empty, leaving him with no fuel to cook with for most of the 7100-mile voyage to Cape Town. To add to his troubles, twelve days out from Newport he found that 136 litres (30 gallons) of engine fuel had leaked into the bilge. Despite being very short of diesel oil now, he tried to make a primitive primus using the engine fuel to heat the tins up. It was not a success, for the contraption belched black smoke everywhere and he eventually had to reconcile himself to eating all his tinned food cold, as well as to cease broadcasting to conserve what little fuel he had left.

The constantly changing winds in the Doldrums tried the patience of all, particularly at night, for each skipper had to remain alert to every change and get up to re-set sails and self-steering gear accordingly. Jeantot's yacht *Crédit Agricole* was equipped with a set of Danavigate 7000 computerized sailing instruments to monitor changes in the true and apparent wind speed, boat speed and compass course. It triggered an alarm when any of the functions increased or decreased beyond the margins that Jeantot decided upon. He found that the electronic alarm built into the equipment was not really loud enough during this leg and had a fire alarm bell fitted during the Cape Town stopover which, reverberating through the spartan alloy hull, made enough din to wake the dead, let alone Jeantot lying less than 3 m (10 ft) away from its bell.

Other skippers relied either on their subconscious intuition to wake them whenever the yacht's motion changed, or a humble alarm clock set to ring at half hour or hourly intervals prompting them to get up and peer through the hatch to check their course and the strength of the wind. Some did oversleep at times though, including Desmond Hampton, who wrote in his diary on 23 September, when he was almost half way to Cape Town: 'The day's run was not helped by the fact that I overslept in the middle of the night and woke to find the wind had done a 180° turn and the boat was heading gently north-west which put me back about 15 miles on my dead reckoned position.' A number of skippers were to find they overslept at times and though nothing untoward happened on this occasion, the problem was to result later in the race in near catastrophe for two competitors and provide a major scare for several others.

As the position reports came in at the end of that fourth week, Jeantot was seen to have extended his lead to more than 1000 miles over the rest of the fleet. With Rodgers forced to lose ground tacking eastwards to clear the bulging land mass of Brazil, the tussle for second place was now between Desmond Hampton, Bertie Reed and Tony Lush.

Reed held the advantage, but 40 miles was all that separated *Gipsy Moth* from the more radical American yacht *Lady Pepperell*, which had now developed a crack at the base of her mizzen mast. The damage was not a major concern at this stage and there was little Lush could do other than mark the extent of the crack, tighten the bolts and hope for the best.

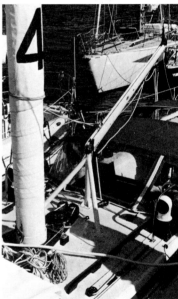

Below: *Lady Pepperell's* two unstayed masts were controlled by continuous lines that led back to the cockpit. Whenever there was a need to change the amount of sail set, the spars could be revolved to wrap or unwrap the loose-footed sails.

Left: The cat-rigged ketch *Lady Pepperell* under sail. Her original glass-fibre masts were replaced by lighter one's of carbon fibre at the end of the first leg.

Another sailor experiencing similar troubles to Lush was the New Zealander Greg Coles aboard the even more radical *Datsun Skyline*, which started out from Newport eleven days behind the fleet. His spar was a deck-stepped revolving wing section that could be moved fore and aft in its step, designed to change the balance of the yacht when sailing at different angles to the wind. Soon after leaving Newport cracks showed up around the base of the carbon fibre mast and though they were to prove superficial, the mere sight of this weakness was enough to make Coles reluctant to sail on port tack.

Another showing disappointment at this stage was Richard McBride, on *City of Dunedin*, which was proving very sluggish in the light variable conditions. Troubles with his hand-made self-steering gear did not help either. 'It must be the only one around that won't steer to windward', he wrote shortly after the start, and finding himself trailing the fleet by as much as 300 miles he entered in his log: 'Those figures speak for themselves. I'm not even in this race. However, racing we are, so we must go on, hoping that the next leg will bring more favourable winds – though a better self-steering gear would help.'

Richard Konkolski aboard *Nike II* finally ran out of luck on his extreme easterly course as he passed through the Cape Verde Islands. 'I've sailed through this area twice before and had always managed to average 160–180 miles a day but this time I didn't get wind for eight bloody days. I tried everything – even two spinnakers set at once to get out of the area,' he told me disconsolately when recounting this first stage of the voyage.

If luck was not on his side, Neptune certainly was for one night while scanning the horizon for a chartered lighthouse to verify his position during this run through the islands, he sailed into an anchorage of fishing craft. Konkolski told me:

> The light from the lighthouse was meant to be very strong – one that could be seen for 20 miles but all I could see were the lights from a village. I was doing 6–7 knots under full genoa and mainsail through the dark when suddenly I saw a shadow pass perhaps half a metre (2 feet) behind the mainsail. It was an anchored fishing boat and I passed so close the keel caught on the anchor line. Then I saw another vessel and immediately ran down and switched off all my lights so that I could see better. It was only then that I realized I was in an anchorage full of fishing boats and could see the surf and the beach very close.

After performing a slalom course of the harbour again, Konkolski finally saw his lighthouse. 'It was just a regular bulb set on a post,' he told me in disgust, and after heading out into the ocean swell he got out a bottle and offered Neptune a drink!

The two American sailors, Dan Byrne and Francis Stokes, sailing traditional production cruisers of similar size had entered this race, like McBride, admitting that they had little chance of winning, but the friendly rivalry that developed between them became a major highlight of the race. Stokes was the more experienced of the two and was expected to stay ahead, but Byrne did his level best to keep up with his mentor throughout the circumnavigation. Approaching the Equator on 25 September, four weeks out from Newport, Stokes held a 175 mile lead over his fellow American and was gliding through the Doldrums almost without pause, his sole distraction being a school of whales. He noted in his diary:

> I was on collision course with four sperm whales this afternoon and was ready to concede right of way as they were rather close. They sheared off and seemed far more interested in their own company than with me. Whales give the impression of being in no hurry. I was going twice as fast. Porpoises on the other hand seem to exude energy, always playing just for the hell of it.

For Byrne, crossing the same 5°N Latitude two days later and facing the Doldrums for the first time, the frustration of finding no wind at all was plain to see from his diary entry. 'CAN'T MOVE THE BOAT' was the only comment on the page. The following 24 hours were very nearly as bad, for *Fantasy* logged no more than 6 miles noon to noon, drawing the brief but heartfelt comment: 'Miserable progress'. The 41 miles covered the following day was a little better, but with Francis Stokes pulling way fast into the South-east Trades, the 10 miles Byrne covered during one eight-hour period was small consolation.

On *Mooneshine*, now at 3°3'N, 24°48'W, Francis Stokes was about to experience far greater worries as his diary entry on 27 September describes so graphically:

> I was squared away on port tack and feeling quite pleased with myself in finding steady wind and breaking out of the Doldrums in good time. I was adjusting lines to prevent chafe, tidying up and generally preparing for about 1200 miles of port tack in steady wind. Wind seemed about 15 knots with occasional sharp waves. I wasn't paying much attention but we went up on one of these, landing pretty hard on the other side. I've done much worse and didn't think too much about it but happened to look up at the port spreader. There was a big gap in the trailing edge where the weld had split open. First you don't want to believe what your eyes are telling you; then you don't want to accept that it has happened to you and not someone else. I ran off and dropped the jib and put the second reef in the main. One backstay had been set up at the time but down to the genoa track. I moved them back to the quarter and set them both up tight. Not really having a plan I put the boat on course jogging along about four knots under staysail and double-reefed main. I talked to *Fantasy*, *Koden* and *Voortrekker* on the 1215 schedule which gave me a chance to assess the possibilities including alternative ports, such as Salvatore.

I decided to try bolting the edge together using the bolts to pull it back into shape. To get up there I lashed ratlines across the lower shrouds working my way up one at a time. That was slow, tough work and took half the afternoon. Drilling and bolting looked feasible, even relatively easy. Hardly any weld was apparent at the break – perhaps ground away for cosmetic reasons. I set the Honda generator in the cockpit, tied the power cord to my belt and went aloft with my bucket of tools. The drilling was slow. Sitting on the spreader was like riding a bucking horse and I was never a horseman. The whole thing took more concentration and concentrated physical effort than almost anything I have done in my sheltered life. Getting five bolts in and drawn up tight took until dark, but it was accomplished without mishap or loss of so much as a washer. I put up a small jib and went below for my ration of rum.

I am fortunate that the weather is easy going and without squalls. I gradually added sail today as I gained confidence in my repair job. I lost 60–80 miles over this affair and goodness knows how much more before Cape Town. *Koden* and *Mooneshine* are the two most southerly boats in Class 2. Others are further east and not so far south and I think (and hope) that will prolong their agony in the Doldrums.

Position reports at the end of the fifth week showed that *Crédit Agricole* was now approximately 1700 miles due east of Cape Town, having extended her lead even further over the fleet. Jeantot could at least see an end to the long windward slog south through the trade wind belt and was about to pick up the prevailing westerlies that would blow him home – according to his calculations – on 12 October. He was now as much as 1200 miles ahead of Bertie Reed, his nearest rival, a lead of such magnitude that some commentators were prompted to recall the footman's famous remark to Queen Victoria after the first America's Cup race round the Isle of Wight: 'Ma'am, there is no second'.

The remainder of the fleet had now split into two groups to tackle the South-east Trades. Those to the west, preferring the easier reaching conditions but longer course skirting round the South Atlantic High were led by local man Reed, now around 180 miles ahead of Hampton and Lush, who had both been slowed by rigging troubles – a broken backstay on *Gipsy Moth*, and a worsening split in *Lady Pepperell*'s mizzen mast. The necessity for *Spirit of Pentax* to tack eastwards to avoid the Brazilian coastline had now put Rodgers out of all contention, and the loss of his yankee sail washed overboard and steering troubles only made matters worse.

Despite the time lost fixing his spreaders, Francis Stokes continued to lead Class 2, for *Mooneshine* was now 90 miles ahead of the larger *Koden Okera V* and a further 200 miles ahead of *Fantasy* and *Skoiern III*. These yachts were all making better headway than those taking the shorter easterly route, led by Richard Broadhead's *Perseverance of Medina*, with Gosson, Bernardin, Konkolski and

Philippe Jeantot arriving at Cape Town to win the first leg with a margin of 6 days and 13 hours.

McBride bringing up the rear.

The two routes were to provide an interesting tactical battle for second place, for within a week, Broadhead, who was suffering problems with his Aries wind vane self-steering gear, was nearly 200 miles closer to Cape Town than Reed, but faced the spider's web of calms within the South Atlantic High. Equally interesting was the struggle for fourth place now developing between Desmond Hampton's *Gipsy Moth V* and Tony Lush on *Lady Pepperell*. Indeed, on 13 October, the same day that Philippe Jeantot crossed the Table Bay finish line to a hero's welcome from hundreds lining the dockside, including the French ambassador, just 28 miles was all that separated these two.

Two days later, when the two were no more than 10 miles apart, a change in the wind provided Hampton with the opportunity to head further south, after Bertie Reed's suggestion during the radio chat show that he should work down to 36°S and stay there until 14°E before cutting up with the current to the finish. 'I will take the local advice,' the British sailor noted in his diary.

Neville Gosson, by now down to his last 14 litres (3 gallons) of fuel and 100 litres (22 gallons) of water, and trailing well behind Broadhead, was having trouble enough just keeping in the race, as can be seen from his diary entry for 17 October, the start of his eighth week at sea:

Well, it was a real disaster today. Forestay broke dropping into the water with the No. 2 genoa quarter furled around it. The secondary 'just-in-case' forestay saved the mast. Some of the Gemini (headfoil) stay plus the large swivel block stayed at the mast top, swinging wildly about on the halyard, smashing into everything. It took five trips up the mast to get it down and I was hit on the head while balancing on the spreader. In the process, the starboard cap shroud has had one strand broken and looks bad. I will try to stay on port tack as much as possible. Have the No 3 genoa hanked onto the outer forestay with the other halyards rigged in support. Hope it holds, but I don't like the chances.

He could now do little more than limp on towards Cape Town, reefing down to a small staysail and double-reefed main whenever the wind increased above 15 knots, and keeping his fingers crossed that the rig would hold up.

On board *Gipsy Moth V*, Desmond Hampton was pondering his next move. On Wednesday 20 October, fifty-three days out from Newport, the winds started to head round towards the east, and by evening he could steer no better than a 60° course. American rival Tony Lush told him during their radio chat that the picture on *Lady Pepperell*'s weather facsimile recorder indicated that the High (which had moved between them and Cape Town) would move away south-east. This, Hampton deduced, would give him north-easterly winds and, if he stayed on the same tack, he would be better placed to take advantage of them if he could climb northwards now.

In his next log entry the following day he was beginning to have doubts about his strategy however:

Altech Voortrekker, Bertie Reed's 14.93-m (49-ft) sloop, the smallest yacht competing in Class 1, racing for the finishing line off Cape Town to take second place.

My plan to take advantage of the NE wind failed. I continued making NE but the wind went hardly north of east and I was stuck at around 34°S, at least a degree too far north. I tacked at noon and started making about 170°M (144°T) but after three hours the wind headed me and I had to tack again. It then continued to veer so that I could make 110°–120°M (084–094°T) and although I was pushed slightly north during the night, the position was tolerable. At best I had wind while *Lady P*, who did the correct thing and tacked south sooner, had none. The result is I am 30 miles closer to Cape Town than her, although she is going to have an easier run in than me from now onwards. My ability to hold onto that lead depends on whether I'm headed and then driven up north by the current. There is everything to play for and it will be very interesting.

The battle for second place between Richard Broadhead and Bertie Reed finally went in the South African's favour with the 14.93-m (49-ft) *Altech Voortrekker* crossing the Cape Town line 6 days 13 hours behind *Crédit Agricole*. Despite the wide gap it was a remarkable achievement when one considers Reed's sixteen-year-old boat was the smallest in Class 1. 'It's like a Mini racing against a Maserati,' exclaimed one onlooker in amazement at the sight of the two yachts lying alongside each other.

Broadhead arrived two days later to take third place after being troubled by leaks and self-steering troubles during the latter part of the voyage. He was followed 12 hours later by fellow Briton Desmond Hampton aboard *Gipsy Moth V* who, though a little despondent at being more than 10 days behind the leader, was overjoyed at finally beating his American rival on *Lady Pepperell* by a sixteen-hour margin.

The distinctive schooner-rigged *Spirit of Pentax* was spotted on the horizon the following dawn but it took Rodgers, who had run out of food and water three days earlier, all day and most of the evening to make it to the line. After lying becalmed for several hours a 50-knot north-easter suddenly sprang up and he spent the day tacking from one side of Table Bay to another, seemingly losing all he had gained every time *Spirit of Pentax* was put about. So bad was the performance of this 16.74-m (55-ft) yacht to windward that Frenchman Jacques de Roux's *Skoiern III*, some 4.27 m (14 ft) shorter than the British yacht, managed to slip through close inshore and cross the line to win Class 2 four hours ahead of Rodgers.

Ten days before, the tussle for Class 2 honours had been very close, for 40 miles was all that had separated De Roux from Yukoh Tada and Francis Stokes, as the three sailed southwards well to the west of the South Atlantic High. Tada was the first to tack eastwards towards Cape Town, and was followed shortly after by Stokes, who caught sight of *Koden Okera V* 5 miles ahead, before both ran into calm. De Roux, on the other hand, held his course for another couple of days and by sailing further south, enjoyed strong winds all the way into Table Bay, to finish a day ahead of Tada and two days ahead of Stokes.

Neville Gosson finally limped in on 30 October, sixty-three days after the start, and was followed the next week by Dan Byrne, Richard Konkolski and Guy Bernardin, with Richard McBride bringing up the rear on 10 November, three days before the fleet were due to start on the second leg, having been at sea for seventy-four days.

Paul Rodgers finished the first leg without food or water; the sandwiches handed to him shortly after he had crossed the line were the first food he had eaten for 4 days. From Cape Town onwards BOC's local companies provided the contestants with all their food supplies at each of the ports of call.

The routes taken by competing yachts on each of the
four legs (second leg, pp. 106–7; third leg, pp. 144–5;
fourth left, p. 158) have been charted from recorded
positions, represented by the dots.
The abbreviations used on the charts are as follows:

CA *Crédit Agricole*
CITY *City of Dunedin*
DAT *Datsun Skyline*
FAN *Fantasy*
GLAD *Gladiator*
GM *Gipsy Moth V*
KO *Koden Okera V*
LADY *Lady Pepperell*
LEDA *Leda Pier One*
MOON *Mooneshine*
NIKE *Nike II* (*Nike III*)
PERS *Perseverance of Medina*
RAT *Ratso II*
SK *Skoiern III*
SPIR *Spirit of Pentax*
AV *Altech Voortrekker*

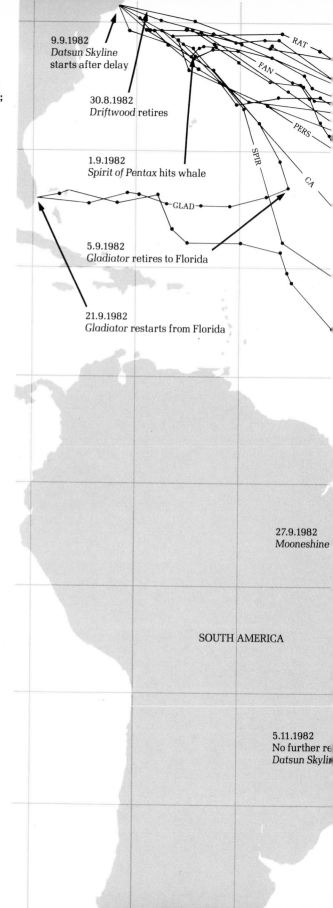

9.9.1982
Datsun Skyline
starts after delay

30.8.1982
Driftwood retires

1.9.1982
Spirit of Pentax hits whale

5.9.1982
Gladiator retires to Florida

21.9.1982
Gladiator restarts from Florida

RAT

FAN

PERS

SPIR

CA

GLAD

27.9.1982
Mooneshine

SOUTH AMERICA

5.11.1982
No further re
Datsun Skyli

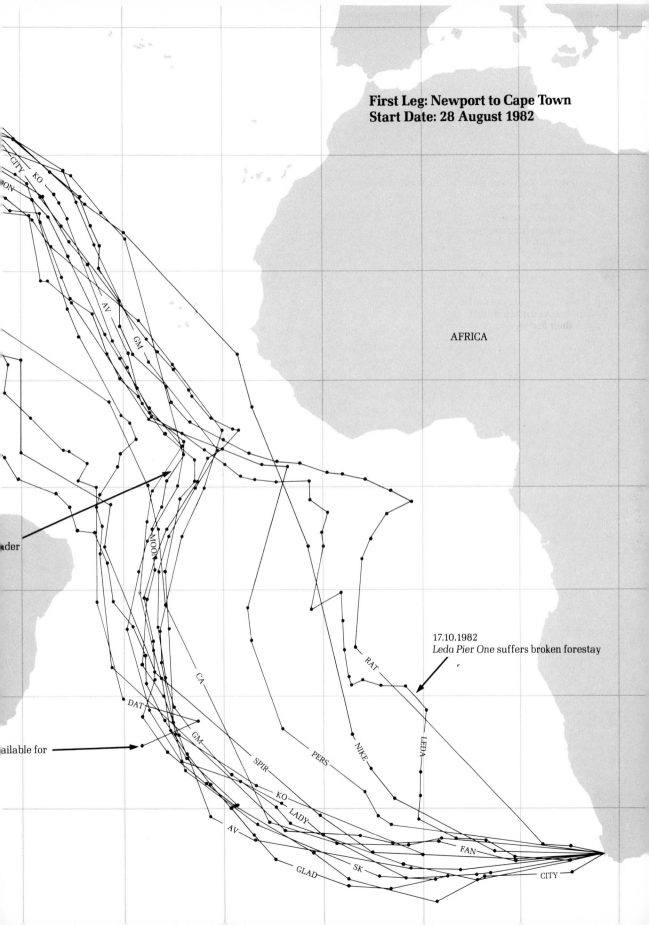

First Leg: Newport to Cape Town
Start Date: 28 August 1982

AFRICA

17.10.1982
Leda Pier One suffers broken forestay

Second Leg:
Cape Town to Sydney

For Richard McBride, it became a race against time to prepare himself and his small yacht in the three short days that remained before the start of the difficult second 6900-mile leg to Sydney. The long hours spent at the helm after *City of Dunedin*'s self-steering gear had failed had left his fingers almost locked around the tiller by the time he arrived at this 'Tavern of the Seas', and exhaustion showed across his face. The rules did in fact allow him to stay in port a full seven days without incurring a time penalty – a decision, as it turned out, that would have been to his advantage; but having sweated so hard to get to the Cape in time to leave with the rest of the fleet, he couldn't bear to let them depart without him.

Richard Konkolski wanted to set sail with them too, but an injury to his back on the eve of the start forced him to remain ashore for a further four days. He was soon rejoined by Paul Rodgers whose departure was delayed overnight by a faulty halyard winch, a problem that only came to light while his yacht was being towed out to sea.

American Dave White, who lost more than two weeks on the fleet by retiring to Florida before deciding to repair the cracked bulkheads on *Gladiator* and continue in the race, missed the restart altogether, arriving in Table Bay three hours after the fleet had departed. Another absentee was Greg Coles in *Datsun Skyline* who, still 2000 miles away, was staggering this way and that across the Atlantic as if writing the name of his yacht across the chart in a final bid to appease his sponsor. The Kiwi finally arrived six weeks behind the race leader and though the damage to his carbon fibre mast proved only superficial and he set out on the second leg, he

Collecting a free ration of beer, supplied by a Cape Town brewery, before the start of the second leg. Left to right: Richard Broadhead, Paul Rodgers, Guy Bernardin and Tony Lush.

soon rejoined White and Rodgers back in Cape Town, with self-steering problems and retired.

During this Cape Town stopover, BOC arranged for each yacht to be fitted with an Argos satellite automatic-position-reporting transponder, similar to those that had already proved their worth in past OSTAR and 2-STAR races. This worldwide weather data and position-fixing satellite collection system, which was to play a crucial role in saving two lives later in the race, was evolved from a co-operative space programme between America and France, involving the American National Aeronautics and Space Administration (NASA), the National Oceanic and Atmospheric Administration (NOAA) and the French Centre National d'Etudes Spatiales (CNES).

Originally developed for use in scientific studies to track the movement of such things as icebergs, polar bears and dolphins, the transponders, looking like small flying saucers fitted to the decks of each yacht, sent their signals automatically to a network of satellites circling the globe ten times daily on polar orbits 800 km (500 miles) into space. The information gained, which included position, atmospheric pressure and ambient temperature, was then retransmitted from the satellites to the ground telemetry stations, two in America and one in France, before being sent via a processing centre in Washington to Toulouse, where the information was decoded ready to be called up at any time by the race organizers.

The Argos satellite system, which picked up and retransmitted automatic position-reporting signals from transponders fitted to each of the yachts.

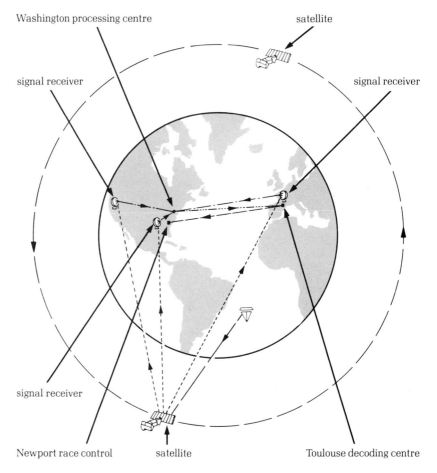

An additional feature which was to prove vital during two Southern Ocean rescues later was the panic switch on each transponder which competitors could operate if they got into difficulties. This activated an emergency signal to alert monitoring staff, first in Toulouse, then Newport, from where the rescue operations were coordinated. Should any competitor have been forced to abandon ship, he could unship the waterproofed transponder, which weighed a mere 6 kg (13¼ lb) and had a battery life of 180 days, from its base and take it with him when he boarded the liferaft, but thankfully that situation never arose, though four skippers were forced to activate the emergency signal before the race was over.

A howling sixty-knot south-easter greeted the competitors when they woke up on Saturday, 13 November, the start day for the second leg, and not one could help but feel some apprehension for what lay ahead. For most, this part of the voyage down through the Roaring Forties and Screaming Fifties was to be a baptism in heavy-weather sailing. If it was blowing force 12 when they set out, what could be in store for them when they went further south?

Before the start of the second leg each of the yachts was fitted, at BOC's expense, with an Argos transponder, which sent out automatic signals, relayed by satellite, indicating position, atmospheric pressure and ambient temperature.

However, just as these gladiators began to emerge with some trepidation from behind the shelter of Cape Town's harbour defences with triple-reefed mainsails and handkerchief-sized jibs, the winds died to a whisper. To observers the sight of this heavily reefed flotilla, struggling against the faintest of breezes seemed strangely at odds with the concept of a race, but with the horizon dark and ruffled with wind, it was obvious that competitors thought they would soon have their hands full once clear of Table Mountain's protective lee.

Those first two hours were frustrating for competitors and supporters alike, and it was only after Richard McBride hoisted his 'green golly' mainstaysail and moved up through the fleet to challenge *Crédit Agricole* that the spell was finally broken. *City of Dunedin*'s performance finally stung others into action, and light reachers sprouted up all around as the fleet gave chase to the early leaders *Altech Voortrekker* and *Leda Pier One*.

As expected, the winds returned with a vengeance later that night and left no one unscathed. One of the first to experience trouble was Richard Broadhead aboard *Perseverance of Medina*. His No 2 genoa ripped as he was rounding Lion's Head, and later he found that much of the green water running across the deck was finding its way below. That night he bucketed out more than 450 litres (100 gallons) swilling around in the bilge.

On *Fantasy*, early rigging problems in the form of a blown genoa and lost halyard, then a fire in the engine ignition, left Don Byrne in despair – and when the cabin bookcase collapsed the next morning, he decided to turn back after covering only 50 miles. 'The worst conditions I have ever experienced at sea,' he wrote in his log. 'I tried all the way back to come up with a reason to drop out. I had had trouble with my back. Perhaps I could say it was giving me too much pain for me to go on. But I couldn't lie, not to my wife. Patricia would encourage me to continue. I knew.' And she did!

Another to be alarmed by the sea's ferocity was Neville Gosson on *Leda Pier One*. That night he wrote in his log: 'Seas becoming phenomenal – I don't think I want to see them in daylight. It would be OK if we were running – but this smashing into it is crazy.

0600: They are as bad in daylight as I'd feared – every now and then a crest breaks over but we are sailing after a fashion – 2 knots forward and 2 sideways.'

Richard McBride gave an even more graphic description. 'The noise was phenomenal, like being in a 44-gallon drum rolling down a gravel road with someone periodically hitting it with a sledge hammer,' he wrote.

On board *Mooneshine*, Francis Stokes was having an equally hard time. With decks continually awash, he decided to lay a-hull and wait for the weather to subside. He wrote in his diary:

Francis Stokes on *Mooneshine* plotting a course to intercept *Lady Pepperell* in order to rescue Tony Lush.

> You lose track of time. I lay on the starboard settee, boots and foul weather gear on, and from time to time looked out for ships and other boats. I don't know if I was asleep but there was a tremendous crash and I felt the boat roll as I was showered with books, canned goods and water which could only have come from the bilge. The G forces are considerable as the boat is struck by a breaking wave and lands with a jolt in the trough. I have no idea whether the mast went in the water – all you know is that something is really wrong when it's black and things are falling on you from God knows where. I rather stupidly picked up a few things before looking out on deck. It was secure out there except for the new hatch dodger which was in shreds. From the deck the waves did not look that menacing, but the wind was certainly hard and there was no thought of putting on sail. It would have been easy and safe to run off but that would have been to the NW and chicken indeed!

There were other scares in store for the 56-year-old American that night too, for he saw the lights of three ships bearing down on him and, with no sail up, felt extremely vulnerable, especially when he drew no response to his warning calls over the VHF radio.

By next morning the weather was no better, and Stokes reckoned he must have been doing very badly so far as the race was concerned. However, after tidying up the mess below he decided that the wind had eased enough to hoist the tri-sail and storm jib. Unfortunately, the easing conditions proved to be a lull. He wrote:

Later the wind blew harder and I made the mistake of lowering the tri-sail – the effect being about the same as lying a-hull. Anyway, I went into the night with just the storm jib and things looked secure enough.

The waves simply did not look dangerous and I slept in the aft cabin with the lee-board in place. At some time in the night, I have no idea when, there was that same awful crash. My head hit the door jamb as I fell out on the floor, really shaken. There was the same mess in the cabin except for the cans of food I had since put in containers, and books flew across the cabin smashing the plywood on the other side. If anything it was a more violent roll than the first – like being in an auto accident, and I was left very sore on the left side.

After recovering from this second capsize, Stokes heard over the radio that Paul Rodgers, who had started a day behind the fleet, and Yokoh Tada had also suffered knockdowns the same night. Like Stokes, Tada was asleep when *Okera V* was thrown over and had taken the full weight of his sewing machine and saxophone which landed on top of him as he lay in his bunk, causing some ugly bruising. 'Was this a "sax assault"?' Richard McBride questioned in his log after Tada had recounted the nightmare. Whatever the case, the little Japanese sailor took no further chances and for the rest of the race he wore a crash helmet whenever he lay down. Once Tada had recovered his senses, he went up on deck and found his mainsail torn to shreds and four gaping holes in the foredeck, marking where the special bowsprit he had fitted in Cape Town to fend off icebergs had been secured before being washed away in the drama.

On *Voortrekker*, Bertie Reed spent much of his second day at sea cleaning out the bilges, after finding more than 20 litres (5 gallons) of diesel had leaked out through a fractured breathing pipe from his fuel tank. It was annoying, but no more than that, for after plugging up the hole, pouring a tin of emulsifying agent into the bilge and bailing the boat dry, the problem was not given another thought – until a week later when the repercussions almost forced him to pull out of the race.

Also facing trouble during this storm was Neville Gosson, who had spent most of his time during the Cape Town stopover renewing rigging damaged during the first leg. First *Leda*'s pulpit was ripped off by the pounding waves to leave lifelines around the deck dangerously slack, then a staysail tore in half, the halyard and head of the sail remaining out of reach, forcing Gosson to climb the mast to retrieve them.

Things were starting to break on *Gipsy Moth*, too. The self-steering vane was the first to snap, followed by the staysail sheet attachment on the end of the main boom, which forced Hampton to climb on deck and take the sail down. Nevertheless, the yacht continued to make good progress, ploughing through the seas under a No 2 jib on a course 40°–50° to the apparent wind, so well that she soon held the lead.

'I suspect some of the others had not got their sea legs by that stage and preferred to lie hove-to,' Hampton said later. 'I should really have put up a storm jib and staysail but those sails were at the bottom of the sail locker forward, and with so much water breaking over the deck, I was worried that if I opened the hatch she would fill up with water.'

Back on *Perseverance*, Richard Broadhead, who was now suffering from saltwater boils caused by his wet clothing, found that he was having to pump the bilge out three times a day to keep pace with the leaking forehatch. To add to his troubles, the bolt rope holding the mainsail in the mast groove had torn, and though he spent several hours restitching the cloth, the problem reappeared almost immediately after the sail had been rehoisted. In the end he was forced to discard it altogether and rely on a second, much smaller mainsail carried as a spare that had seen better days.

During that first week at sea, the succession of gales that swept the fleet uncovered a common problem that was to drive some skippers near to despair before they reached Sydney. The trouble lay with their unreliable self-steering equipment and its inability to keep some yachts on a steady course downwind once wind and sea began to boil.

On *Altech Voortrekker*, Bertie Reed found that his Aries equipment allowed the yacht to yaw 30°–40° off course when sailing on a starboard tack. The problem was most acute when she was surfing for, as the boat was picked up and thrust forward by the wave, the wind pressure on the vane progressively lessened until all control was lost and the yacht rounded up in an uncontrolled broach. Reed swapped the Aries equipment with an identical spare carried as insurance against breakage, but this had no better effect on handling. He also tried to counter the problem by using lengths of shock cord tied with varying tensions to the vane, tiller and servo, but it was all to no avail and in the end he was forced to steer by hand for much of the voyage.

Richard Broadhead had no better luck with his Aries fitted on *Perseverance*. First the steering arm broke during a fifty-knot blast that set his yacht surfing at over fifteen knots. He managed to repair it, but the part broke again the following day and he was left with no alternative but to change over to the Sailormat he carried as a spare. This equipment was even less effective, for the breakaway couplings, designed to save the gear from permanent damage when overloaded, gave out after just three days of light weather use. *Perseverance* was also equipped with a Solent autopilot but this electronic equipment guided by a compass bearing had a high consumption, requiring the batteries to be recharged three hours a day, and Broadhead did not have enough fuel to last all the way to Sydney. This point proved somewhat academic anyway, for the unit packed up within 48 hours, to leave him without any effective method of self-steering. Unable to think of a ready solution, he eventually decided to head towards the Kerguelen Islands under reduced sail, in the hope that someone among the small research community living there might be able to weld up the broken arm on his Aries.

By this time, two weeks out from Cape Town, Bertie Reed was also thinking he would have to head towards land, not because of his self-steering problems, but because of a badly infected right wrist, poisoned by the diesel absorbed into the cuff of his polar wear while he had been cleaning out the bilge the week before. Antibiotics might have cured the infection but he could not recall where they had been stored. Left unchecked, the infection slowly spread up his arm from a swelling the size of a golf ball on his wrist. The pain eventually forced him to ask Alastair Campbell, his ham contact in Durban, if he could find some kitchen remedy to ease the pain and save him from putting in to Amsterdam Island to seek medical help. The next day Campbell came back suggesting the application of a sugar compress over the wound – hardly an orthodox medical solution – but it worked in drawing the poison out. 'The discharge was unreal. I've never seen anything like it', Bertie said in Sydney, with obvious relief. 'It was hard, just like soggy macaroni, and once the last bit came out, the hole in my arm looked like the butt end of a cigarette. For several days I had the use of only one arm, which was bad news when it came to changing sails, but it was fully recovered by the time I reached here.'

The Argos position reports during this period showed that the race was proving to be a much closer fight than many had expected. Philippe Jeantot may have held a modest 70-mile lead that second Saturday, but throughout the previous week there had been little to divide *Crédit Agricole* from *Gipsy Moth V*, further to the south. Given the headwinds they were facing, *Gipsy Moth V* was just as likely to recapture the lead again once the current 'low' had passed overhead. Despite his problems, Bertie Reed was also in there fighting, lying a close third no more than 30 miles behind the British yacht.

'Unbelievable,' Hampton wrote of the conditions. 'The wind continued easterly and increased to forty knots plus thick fog. My views on the matter are unprintable. If I had wanted to beat into a 40-knot wind for days on end in freezing fog, I would have sailed the other way round the world.'

Feelings on *Crédit Agricole* were similar. Jeantot entered in his log:

> The whole day is spent trying to make the boat go faster. I am tacking to windward trying to be always on the good side, but that was a mistake. I should have gone south. I would have got some speed rather than heading into the wind. *Gipsy Moth* and *Voortrekker* have both caught up with me and *Gipsy Moth* is

Crédit Agricole **under cutter rig in the Roaring Forties. Unexpected headwinds slowed the leaders and allowed the smaller yachts, sailing in reaching winds on a lower latitude, the chance to catch up.**

even ahead. I had better put some coal in the furnace!

It can't go on like this. I like *Gipsy Moth* – but behind me … let's get going, *Crédit Agricole*.

In fact I am surprised that Desmond is doing so well on this second leg for he could not make any headway during the first. He is obviously putting all he's got into it and it surprises me. It is proving to be much more of a contest.

These unexpected headwinds resulted from a strong high-pressure system which developed over the Indian Ocean dropping further south than usual to affect the normal westerly air-stream in the Roaring Forties. So strong was its influence that even a deep depression, that dropped barometer readings down to 992 mb as it swept across the fleet that weekend, failed to have any impact. This resulted in the leaders facing headwinds for a week and allowed the smaller yachts, sailing in reaching winds on a lower latitude further astern, the chance to catch up some lost ground. Not that this necessarily made conditions any easier for them, for the winds, gusting between forty and fifty knots, piled up the seas, their boiling crests making progress an extremely hazardous affair. Guy Bernardin aboard *Ratso II*, the smallest yacht in the fleet, was probably having the worst time.

'The boat is not really designed for that type of sea. It is too light, too much like a dinghy, so I have to trim it well all the time otherwise it goes everywhere,' he explained later. 'The self-steering could not cope at all in wind strengths of forty knots or more, and I had to steer – or rather fight with the tiller – all the time in order to keep her on course.'

Sailing without sleep for forty-eight hours, Bernardin's concentration finally lapsed and the little 11.58-m (38-ft) craft suffered her first knockdown. It was a scary few moments, but as the wave receded, *Ratso* popped back up again almost unscathed, with the Frenchman wiser but none the worse from the ordeal.

Tony Lush, holding seventh place, did not have the same good fortune when his larger Class 1 boat *Lady Pepperell* also succumbed in the stormy conditions that day. Indeed, he was lucky to get away with his life.

'At the time I was doing four to six knots under bare poles. It was dark and as things were looking under control, I went below to take a nap. I was awake when the wave hit and remember, as I lay in my bunk, looking past my toes and seeing a kaleidoscope of items fly through the air as the boat went over. I think she was sailing down a wave on a very broad reach when the crest broke, throwing the boat into a sort of swan dive with a third twist, rolling her over through about 135°,' is how he described the incident later. Initially the 16.46-m (54-ft) yacht looked undamaged. Her carbon-fibre masts stepped during the stopover in Cape Town were left intact, a fact the other sailors found remarkable, and apart from the mess below, all that required attention was the sat/nav aerial which had become disconnected. Or so it seemed until first light the next morning, when the full extent of the damage was realized.

'Then I saw why the floorboards over the keel were out of place. The reinforcement inside the hull supporting the keel had broken away,' Lush told me. 'When I first looked in the keel sump I thought it was the strainer moving around, but on closer inspection I realized it was the keel that was moving from side to side through a 20° arc, which was very disheartening to say the least. There was no way I could fix the boat, and after looking at the pilot chart and seeing Australia was still a very long way away, all I could do was start edging up north and with the idea of heading back to Durban.'

Later he sent out an emergency PAN message. Conditions were not good and he failed to get any response from Cape Town Radio – which was nothing less than expected, for, like others in this fleet, he had been unable to raise this commercial station since leaving South Africa. However, Alastair Campbell, the ham enthusiast monitoring the fleet in Durban, did read him – just – and passed his message via fellow ham Rob Koziomkowski, in Newport, to Race Control. Luckily, weather conditions began to subside the following morning and propagation was also better, for when Lush turned his radio set on, the first thing he heard was Francis Stokes and Alastair Campbell discussing his plight.

Rob Koziomkowski, a ham radio operator based in Newport, Rhode Island, started in an informal way as a communication link with Greg Coles but later became the lynchpin of communications passing between the fleet and race control. He was to play a vital role in rescue operations.

Opposite: Philippe Jeantot, a 30-year-old oil-rig diver from Concarneau in France, led the race from start to finish.

'How are you, Francis?' Tony butted in, which Stokes found rather funny, considering that it was Lush who was in trouble. The latest Argos positions passed to them by Campbell showed *Mooneshine* then 50 miles ahead, to be the nearest to Lush and his stricken yacht, which by now was taking on water at the rate of 10 litres (2 gallons) a minute.

'I gave Tony an ultimatum,' Stokes said later about the radio conversation. 'Either he had to abandon his boat, or go on alone, and with the problems he had, it didn't take long for him to make up his mind!'

Rather than turn about, Stokes decided to remain hove-to and wait for Lush to sail down to him. Alastair passed on the next set of Argos position fixes fed to him by Dave White co-ordinating the rescue from his yacht moored in Cape Town. Although the figure for *Lady Pepperell* matched her sat/nav reading, *Mooneshine*'s position, for an unexplained reason, was as much as 30 miles adrift, so Stokes turned to his sextant instead for a more accurate fix. It was the right decision too, for eight hours after the rescue had begun, just before dusk, he caught sight of *Lady Pepperell*'s distinctive rig in the setting sun about 3 miles off. 'Bear left 10° and come on in,' he called over the radio to his fellow American, and shortly afterwards the two made their rendezvous. 'We were very lucky,' Stokes remarked later. 'It would have been just as easy to miss him.'

As the yachts came alongside, two lines were thrown across for Lush to haul himself and his gear across. First came a bag containing clothes, sleeping bag and cameras, together with a well-protected bottle of J & B Scotch and a sacred copy of Joshua Slocum's book *Sailing Alone around the World* that he had taken with him on all his trips. The American also packed his antibiotics just in case Bertie Reed's infected arm created a second emergency and Stokes was called on again to assist. Once this had been hauled across safely, Lush, a non-swimmer, donned his life jacket and safety harness before pulling himself hand over hand across the 150-ft gap.

Once alongside, Stokes was quick to help Lush out of the near-freezing water, then left him to strip off in the cockpit, as he cut the two boats apart and set a storm jib before joining his new-found companion in a celebratory nip from that Scotch bottle.

Rescued and rescuer. Tony Lush, who had been saved from the sinking *Lady Pepperell*, standing in the companionway and Francis Stokes at the wheel of *Mooneshine* when they arrived at Sydney Harbour at the end of the second leg.

Left: Problems with the mast step of *Lady Pepperell* stopped Tony Lush from setting her mizzen in anything but very light conditions in the latter part of the leg to Cape Town.

Left: Self-steering problems on *City of Dunedin* forced Richard McBride to stay at the helm much of the time in the latter stages of the first leg.

Opposite: *City of Dunedin* passing through the Sargasso Sea, a relatively still area of the North Atlantic north-east of the West Indies where large drifts of *Sargassum* weed float on the surface.

Left: Yukoh Tada contrived to photograph his yacht, *Koden Okera V*, and himself by mounting his camera on an extension pole.

Perfect conditions for the arrival of *Perseverance of Medina* in Table Bay. As did most of the competitors, Richard Broadhead relied on a spinnaker sock, seen at the head of the sail, to control this running sail when hoisting and recovering.

Inset: Jacques de Roux and Yukoh Tada, winner and runner-up of the Class 2 of the first leg, at the prize-giving in Cape Town.

Right: Richard McBride's *City of Dunedin*, a heavy steel yacht, only performed well in strong conditions.

Opposite: *Crédit Agricole* fast reaching under double-headed rig.

Below: Yukoh Tada on *Koden Okera V* preparing a dish of seaweed and flying fish during the first leg.

Right: Four of the skippers in Sydney. Left to right: Bertie Reed, Neville Gosson, Philippe Jeantot and Jacques de Roux. Gosson and de Roux completed the second leg within 4½ hours of each other, to take third and fourth places respectively.

Below: Pier One, built close by Sydney Harbour Bridge and now an old-world amusement centre, played host to the yachts at the end of the second leg.

Another to decide that he had taken enough punishment at the end of the second week was Jacques de Roux, whose 13.11-m (43-ft) *Skoiern III* had until then been making quite remarkable progress, holding fourth place overall, well ahead of her Class 2 rivals. In a radio call to *Gipsy Moth*, he told Desmond Hampton that his self-steering rudder had been damaged beyond repair in the wild conditions that prevailed, forcing him to head up towards Reunion Island. 'This is sad as he was doing rather well,' Hampton wrote in his diary. 'Some people seem to have all the bad luck. I hope mine holds.' Later, however, once other competitors had warned him about the cyclones that he could expect further to the north, de Roux decided to continue in the race, making a temporary repair to the foil.

After the batterings received the previous week, conditions treated the fleet more kindly during their third week at sea, the milder weather allowing the Class 1 leaders to turn in some remarkable runs as well as give those with damage time to make and mend. Philippe Jeantot continued to keep Hampton at bay – but only just. Passing the halfway mark to Sydney with a flying seven-day run of 1437 miles, an average of more than eight knots – later acknowledged as a record for a single-handed monohull during a circumnavigation – the Frenchman drew 120 miles ahead of his rival, despite losing his spinnaker when *Crédit Agricole* suffered a severe knockdown in the uneven swell off the Kerguelens.

In spite of his steering problems and his infected arm, Bertie Reed continued to hold on to third place, trailing Hampton 280 miles, but three days of slow progress finally robbed de Roux of his fourth place, which was taken over by Neville Gosson. Setting *Leda Pier One* on a course further south, he managed to overtake two yachts during his 1286-mile week's run along the shorter course. To the outside world it appeared that things were at last looking up for this determined Aussie. Unfortunately, the picture onboard was very different, for the rigging problems Gosson had suffered on the first leg continued to plague his progress now. First, the Gemini headsail furling gear broke, followed by the forestay (newly fitted in Cape Town) ten days into the voyage, and thereafter each time he solved one set of problems he merely created others. 'With no forestay to hank the headsails to, all the strain was taken in their head and tacks with the result that these corners started pulling out of the sails,' he explained. 'When I solved this by bolting metal plates over the attachment points, the loads were merely transmitted onto the halyards with the result that the tails started to break. At one point I lost four halyards one after the other. It was just an endless process of tearing and repairing sails.'

Writing in his log at the end of that third week at sea, Gosson said:

Well, up went the staysail again at 0230 hrs. Let's hope that's the last time for repairs to that sail.

Neville Gosson's *Leda Pier One* suffered rig problems throughout the race, much of the rigging being over seven years old.

It is so cold. I would like to climb the mast and renew a spinnaker halyard but by the time I get half way up, my hands are frozen and I cannot hang on. I nearly fell when I cut down the staysail a few days ago and that is only three-quarters of the way up! I will come back to lat. 50° and see if the weather improves. I hope so!

Reed and Broadhead's self-steering problems continued to affect their performances, the South African going so far as to estimate the distance lost on leaders as 10–20 miles a day. 'There are a few pages in this log that have not got many entries. All I can say is that if I ever again experience these problems with self-steering I'll head for the nearest port!' he wrote in obvious disgust.

Five days after changing course towards the Kerguelens in the hope of finding a welder to repair the broken steering arm on his Aries unit, Broadhead, who had been hand-steering for twelve hours at a time, suddenly had a brainwave:

0830 GMT: Hand steering and suddenly it comes to me how to fix the Aries! Can use two pieces of aluminium to hold the block and a bit of rope on the opposite arm to act as a stop. Simple, but it has taken five days to think of the solution.

1400 GMT: Have fixed the Aries – I hope it will last. The rope stop will need tightening daily to take up stretch.

Change course and head for Sydney!!

During the fourth week at sea, the moderate conditions changed for the worse once more, to batter all but the two leaders who were now nearing the Australian continent.

The first to fall once again was Guy Bernardin's *Ratso II*, which suffered another severe knockdown on Monday, 6 December. The next day her wind vane and wheel steering broke, forcing the Frenchman to remain in the cockpit and grapple with the emergency tiller poking out through the aft companionway hatch for the rest of the voyage.

The same day, Richard Broadhead heard on the radio that *Skoiern III* had also suffered a second knockdown this time through 180°, which had thrown de Roux out of his bunk and caused his fuel tank to rupture. On Wednesday it was Richard McBride's turn, and as the winds gusted over 50 knots he wrote in his log:

Bloody amazing scene out there. Seas going in all directions including over us. I must admit that this was an experience of some magnitude and one that I greeted with mixed feelings. We have now reached that point where the situation is beyond control, chaos reigns and the rational world of order and symmetry are but a fond memory.

You may wonder if it's so bad, how come I am writing this. Well, after twelve hours of full gale, the seas have lengthened out so much that between being pummelled by breakers there are intervals of relative peace when the only indication of impending nastiness is the noise in the rigging – a steady shriek. The boat shudders a little from time to time, nervously waiting the next onslaught. A couple of seas slip by with little apparent effect, a quick roll each way, a bit of a slap on the side from an erratic crest, then into the trough as the next series of big ones get ready for the attack. A look out the hatch reveals bedlam. From the top of the swell one looks astern, into the west where the gale is blowing from, and all one sees is a series of huge white crests breaking and going in all different directions.

Yesterday, before the westerly blow, there were conflicting winds from the S-W and N-W, force 6–7. These cross airflows generated big confused seas. It seems as if the yacht was the focal point of two intersecting lines of moving hills. The westerly swell has mostly overridden these other swells but their effects are still felt. When all three crests come together, a mighty column of water rises up and crashes. When this happens, we really take a beating. We generally take the onslaught on the port quarter, meaning we head north of east. It's almost impossible and unwise to attempt to steer down-wind.

As the big seas approach, the stern lifts and the boat speeds up a little, then dips the starboard rail. It seems impossible that she'll lift in time but each time she does and no solid water comes over the stern (everywhere else though). Often the breaker catches the stern and slews us round. The vane goes over but usually straightens quickly. Sometimes, the wind pins us down and the rudder loses its bite and it takes a minute or two to come round.

The next wave may catch us and bury us in foam or green water – the noise associated with the latter is awe-inspiring, like mighty cannon fire. Sometimes, she catches the wave and if our sections were flatter, we'd surf. We are a little heavy for that. But we ride the crest and each stanchion creates its own bow wave. She moves swiftly till the wave roars on ahead and drops us in the following trough. The amazing thing about these seas is the speed at which they move.

Usually though, we are thrown about like a piece of flotsam, rolling one way then the other, dipping port rail then starboard, water rushing along the side deck and pouring over the lee coamings into the cockpit. From there it joins the sea via the huge cockpit drains.

Inside the cabin the comparative peace that exists between assaults is broken either by a massive roar and roll to leeward, or by a succession of wild rolls making everything airborne below deck. I see the windward porthole covered in water as I perch on the lee bunk. When a particularly bad wave hits, a jet of water squirts in the sliding hatch cover. Its bad enough sitting here, but watching it happen ...

We could be rolled over. That's not such a wild idea. We heard that *Skoiern* turned 180 degrees yesterday but didn't sustain much damage, luckily.

What procedure should one take under these conditions?
1. 'Heave to' and head into the gale?
2. 'Lying a hull' under bare poles with the threat of being rolled sideways?
3. 'Running with it before the wind towing a sea anchor?'
4. 'Keep sailing,' surely right, and use boat speed to give a little stability?

The next day, however, *City of Dunedin* succumbed.

10.20. After updating the log, we were knocked down with our masts in the water. The dark blue-black ocean was visible through the cabin sky light. And everything, absolutely everything tumbled about the cabin as if in a concrete mixer. I was seated on the weather berth with my feet braced against the table loading a film into the camera. With no warning that I observed, the boat lurched and I swung on the handrail pole adjacent to the coal stove with my feet hung in mid-air above the table.

I watched with amazement and fear as everything piled up on the port side. Unfortunately, the settee had been pulled out for sleeping so all the carefully stored cans made a dive through the air, leaving their dents on the kauri table. The noise was deafening. The incident seemed to go for an age but in reality it was only seconds. The boat lurched back upright, but it took me longer to regain my equilibrium.

During the afternoon I steered most of the time. Every so often, I would rush below to warm up and clear up a little until the motion got too wild and I would have to return to the tiller. The dome is of no value in these conditions – visibility is poor and it steams up, reducing vision even further.

It was during one of these spells that a potentially far more dangerous situation occurred. A sea of epic proportions, much larger than I had yet observed, came barrelling up behind, forming a real vertical wall. As I leaned over higher than the masthead, I watched in awe, and gripped the tiller with such tenacity, realizing I could not avoid this dousing.

The ship pointed down as the stern rode up till it seemed we would fall frontwards. But the sea broke. As it pinned us, the log hit ten knots. With all the water dumped, it sluiced aft, dragging me out the cockpit and held me down as it tried to strain me through the mainsheet frame and pushpit.

The force and power of the water was indescribable. It all showed just how vulnerable one is on board even in a cockpit. Thank goodness, I'm a born coward. When it's really rough, I open the hatch door, reach out and grab the safety line, hook on, then go on deck.

To add insult to injury, I had no sooner changed into dry clothes, when I opened the cockpit hatch just a whisker, having ascertained that all seemed quiet, and about ten gallons of water poured in on me. More wet gear!

On *Perseverance*, the windspeed indicator seemed perpetually locked against its stop at sixty knots and Richard Broadhead, knowing that if he used his self-steering in these fearsome conditions it was likely to break again, was steering by hand for twelve hours before resting up while the yacht lay hove-to.

Describing the conditions he told me: 'Every ten minutes or so the seas rolled back into vertical walls and once I nearly pitchpoled. The seas were huge, as high as the mast, and as the bow buried up to the forehatch, I just sat at the wheel holding on for grim death looking almost vertically down the boat as she started to go over. Then as the wave broke, the bow came up and she surfed off with the whole deck underwater. All I could see was the bloody wheel in front of me and the mast and rigging standing up through the surf. I would say she was doing 30 knots plus, there was a hell of a lot of power, and if I had had any sail up she would definitely have gone over.'

Meanwhile, approximately one thousand miles ahead, Bertie Reed, now trailing *Gipsy Moth* by a 200-mile margin, was no less exposed to the storms. *Altech Voortrekker*'s anemometer had been fluctuating around force 6 for much of the past week, and with steering problems almost as bad as those on Broadhead's boat, the

South African was having an equally hard time. However, reading his log entry for that day, it was obvious he had not lost any of that competitive spirit.

0440 GMT: Position 42°10′S. 116°28′E.

Still a big sea. Sunny with a few clouds overhead. *Crédit Agricole* had 10 knots of wind during the night and I caught him by 60 miles.

11.45 GMT: Second reef taken in. Dark clouds again. Last night I found that these squalls bring thirty knots plus. We've been going well considering that the Aries is still not doing its job. At this rate it looks like being the 23rd (December) in Sydney. I look forward to it.

16.00 GMT: Down No 2 (genoa). Wind thirty-five knots. Doing eight knots with reefed main. What a night. Knocked over with stanchions in water. Mountainous sea and gale force wind. It's supposed to be fun!

The day before *Voortrekker*'s knockdown, Neville Gosson, steering a shorter course 11° further south, had reduced the South African's third place lead to little more than 70 miles and Gosson was hoping that the next depression might push *Leda Pier One* ahead. 'What happens when the barometer reaches a steady 967 mb. Well, we are about to find out. I have never seen such a low reading,' Gosson wrote in his log.

Alas, it was to bring more bad luck, for instead of the expected westerlies, the wind turned east and for three days he was faced with a force 6 right on the nose, leaving him with no alternative but to head even further south.

'I just cried because it put us right out of the race,' he admitted later, 'It was the final straw and I didn't think I could take any more. Everything that could have gone wrong on that leg did go wrong. It was as if someone up there was testing me to see when I would break. That easterly was the breaking point and I just cried out: "All right. I give in. Now give us some good stuff." '

Those easterlies stayed for three days, and without a forestay to support the mast or hank his headsail to, *Leda* could make little progress towards Sydney and instead got pushed south to 55° 42′S.

Up ahead, 85 miles was all that divided Jeantot's *Crédit Agricole* and Hampton's *Gipsy Moth* at the end of that fourth week at sea, the two maxis having put 1224 and 1259 miles under their respective keels, leaving the French boat with less than 1300 miles to Sydney. Even more remarkable, considering the knockdown he suffered earlier in the week, was the 1168 miles covered by Jacques de Roux, on *Skoiern III*, which put him back in third place some 30 miles nearer to Bass Strait than Gosson and firmly in control of Class 2 once more. Lying in sixth place within the fleet, *Perseverance* had now dropped 1300 miles behind the leader and was followed by *City of Dunedin*, which had a 50-mile lead over *Mooneshine* with *Ratso*, *Nike*, *Koden Okera* and *Fantasy* bringing up the rear.

Neville Gosson, who set off for the race from Australia clean-shaven.

The smaller Class 2 boats were now more than halfway but still far from being in the clear, as the events the following Wednesday were to prove. Fast dropping barometers on all the boats provided the first indications of yet another storm and some, now 'gun-shy' after earlier knockdowns, were quick to reduce sail. On *Perserverance*, Broadhead was faced with force 5 easterly headwinds for six hours and but for a keen eye might easily have lost his rig.

> 0800 GMT: Split pin on forestay screw clevis pin shears off and the clevis pin is three-quarters of the way out. Take down all sail. Slacken forestay and replace. It has bent the bottlescrew — came close to losing forestay.

It was a day Broadhead will probably always remember, for he also had to repair the Aries self-steering twice and cope with the pulpit which sheered loose.

On *City of Dunedin*, Richard McBride, who suffered badly bruised ribs after being thrown by the seas against a winch, was coping with a broken mast step and self-steering, but this was nothing compared to the problems Bernardin was facing on *Ratso*. At 9.00 GMT, night time in the Southern Ocean, he had been forced to heave-to after a lengthy fight with his emergency tiller to keep his yacht on an even keel in the force 8/9 conditions that prevailed. Seven hours later, as the storm began to recede and when waves are often at their worst, a huge roller, its crest boiling, totally overwhelmed the small aluminium craft.

> When I saw the wave coming, I grabbed the winch with my arm but as the water swept down rolling the boat through about 160° I felt my feet leaving the cockpit and my arm slipping from the winch. I felt as if I was in space. Everything was white and green. It was beautiful — the greatest moment in my life.
>
> Once I realized I was no longer in the boat I lashed out to find anything to hold on to and was lucky to grasp the running backstay as the boat came up again, and dropped back into the cockpit.

There is no doubt that the Frenchman was lucky to survive, but he was brought back to earth quickly enough first by the pain in his bruised leg, then by the sight of the carnage around him. On deck, the main compass had been washed away and ropes were a tangled mass, but down below the mess was even worse. The liferaft had landed in his bunk, and the many items of loose gear, including the radio mike, were now swilling around in all the water that had poured in through the open hatch. It took him two hours to bail the yacht out, and many more to tidy up, but miraculously the radio microphone, normally so susceptible to salt-water corrosion, still worked, once it had been dried out.

Around this time all radio contact was lost with Richard Konkolski, who until this point had been making steady ground on the Class 2 leaders since his delayed start from Cape Town. Concern became all the greater when *Nike*'s Argos plots, which had begun to show a slower pace, also indicated that he had changed course towards Fremantle, but the full extent of his problems remained unknown until the Czech docked at this West Australian port on Boxing Day. ˙

Arriving with broken rigging, torn sails and a seized engine, the exhausted sailor had been forced to hand-steer his 13.41-m (44-ft) yacht for 2500 miles after suffering a bad broach at the beginning of December. For the rest of the voyage he was forced to stay at the wheel for eighteen hours at a time, then let the boat drift for a further six while he rested, and by the time he arrived he was suffering from badly swollen limbs and circulatory problems.

The knockdown came while Konkolski was charging his batteries and he immediately rushed on deck to get the genoa down, but another headsail stowed on deck ready hanked to the forestay filled with water and the added strain broke the forestay. He heard the engine falter shortly after. With the yacht pinned down on her side by the wind, oil had drained out of the sump leaving the bearings to run dry, which left him without any means of generating electricity. And electricity was crucial, for *Nike* was equipped only with an electronic self-steering system, for lack of funds had precluded Konkolski from fitting a wind-vane back-up before the start.

In Fremantle, friends he had made during a previous voyage helped to repair his sails and rigging, and also provided him with a small generator so that he could continue on to Sydney, but the diversion cost him all chance of winning the race.

Philippe Jeantot was the first to reach Bass Strait, rounding King Island in the evening of 16 December, thirty-four days from Cape

Left: *Crédit Agricole* arriving off Sydney Heads under two heavy-weather 'booster sails', boomed out running sails with their luffs set in the twin-grooved headfoil, which Jeantot used to steady the yacht downwind when conditions in the Southern Ocean became too much for a spinnaker.

Right: Philippe Jeantot celebrating his success in winning the second leg.

Town, having extended his significant lead over Desmond Hampton to 120 miles during the previous week. Apart from a spinnaker wrapped round the forestay during the run through Bass Strait, which took him five hours to clear, the Frenchman had an uneventful run up the Australian coast to Sydney and a rain-soaked but rousing reception. *Crédit Agricole* crossed the finish line inside Sydney Heads at 9.15 local time on Sunday, 19 December, thirty-five days nine hours and fourteen minutes after leaving Cape Town. It was another magnificent victory, but marred by the news, learned as he sailed through the Heads, of the tragedy that had befallen Desmond Hampton and *Gipsy Moth* V the previous morning.

The Englishman, who had been the only man to pose any threat

Gipsy Moth V wrecked on the rocks of Gabo Island, 250 miles from the Sydney finishing line.

Desmond Hampton salvaged what he could from the stricken *Gipsy Moth V*, using a chainsaw to cut out winches and deck fittings.

to Jeantot during any stage of the 6900-mile voyage, had run aground on Gabo Island, 250 miles from the Sydney finish line and *Gipsy Moth* had been wrecked. It shocked the Frenchman just as much as the British public, who woke that morning to find the dramatic photographs of the late Sir Francis Chichester's wrecked yacht splashed across the front pages of their newspapers.

Hampton, who had been awake for more than twenty-four hours as he threaded a course past the many oil rigs to the north of Bass Strait, had lain down for a well-earned hour's rest, overslept, and only woke as the yacht ran ashore after being sent off course by a shift in the wind.

The first thought to flash through his mind on waking was that one of her masts had fallen down, but the moment he poked his head up through the hatch, the awful truth dawned. Rushing on deck, he hurriedly pulled down the sails then started the engine to reverse off, only to find that the folding prop chose that moment to stay firmly closed. Then, as Hampton fought with the control lever, the yacht slipped further along the rocks, pivoted on her bows, then drifted stern first into a crevice where she lodged hard under the shadow of Gabo Island's lighthouse. Soon after, there was a further sickening crunch as the rudder and propshaft snapped off, and from that moment on *Gipsy Moth* was doomed.

Hampton rushed below to transmit a Mayday over the radio, then pushed the panic button on his Argos transponder to alert the world of his plight, before jumping ashore and running up to the lighthouse keepers' house for help. With such a large hole in *Gipsy Moth*'s bows, he needed a pump, fast, if he was to stand any chance of saving this famous yacht, but though the two lighthouse keepers, Ted and Ray, made more than twenty telephone calls around the island, each drew a blank. The Englishman had to admit defeat.

All he could do was rescue what was salvageable from the stricken yacht. Helped by the lighthouse keepers and a small group of sailors that had been alerted by the distress signals, he worked until dark to cut away all her deck gear and equipment with a chainsaw, starting again at first light the following morning to complete the job. By midday all that remained onboard *Gipsy Moth* were her masts and one foresail; her winches, the deck hatches, radio and instruments had all been stripped out before the yacht was finally left to her fate.

How did this disaster occur? 'I was tired and simply overslept,' Hampton said later in Sydney. 'I had been awake for much of the previous twenty-four hours threading *Gipsy Moth* past the many oil rigs to the north of Bass Strait, before lying down for an hour's rest. I normally slept for an hour at a time, then got up to check the boat, but this time I slept for an hour and three-quarters. That's not an excuse, single-handers don't have excuses, but while I slept, the following winds must have swung round and pushed me off course.'

Less than 400 m (1200 ft) was all that divided 'Gipsy Moth's course from the open sea and a narrow escape past this barren outcrop that marks the south-eastern extremity of Australia's mainland, but luck was not on Hampton's side. 'She just drove in head first doing about eight-and-a-half knots, putting a great hole in her nose,' he said.

Hampton immediately accepted full responsibility for the loss of the eleven-year-old yacht and also defended the course through the notorious Bass Strait, criticized as being too dangerous by fellow British competitor Paul Rodgers. Before the start from Cape Town, Rodgers had called for a change in the course that would have taken the fleet round Tasmania to reduce the risk of running aground, but Hampton said, after being reunited with his wife and children in Sydney: 'We all knew the course before the race started. We all knew of the danger and had weighed up the risks.'

Instead of blaming circumstances for the grounding, Hampton reflected with obvious enthusiasm on the fantastic race he had had for the lead against Philippe Jeantot, who had averaged more than eight knots during this Southern Ocean leg. For the first two weeks, there had been little to divide the two of them as they vied for the lead, and it was only after conditions moderated south of Amsterdam Island that the lighter *Crédit Agricole* finally pulled ahead. Hampton called it the most demanding sailing he had ever done, saying, 'I needed everything in terms of strength, mental resilience and determination to keep the pressure up. The decision not to set an extra sail was always the easy option, but with Jeantot always so close I had to make every effort to increase speed, even though this increased discomfort.'

With this second loss in the race, Bertie Reed, now nursing a broken toe after catching his foot under one of the solar panels mounted on *Altech Voortrekker*'s deck, moved into second place, finishing forty-two hours behind the Frenchman. He was followed eight days later by Neville Gosson, who was down to his last two headsails, supported on makeshift halyards made up from knotted spinnaker sheets. He completed the course four-and-a-half hours ahead of Class 2 leader Jacques de Roux after the closest of races up the Australian coastline.

Gosson, who had again run out of gas before the finish and so had no means of heating his Christmas lunch, decided to make the 80-mile detour round Tasmania to avoid the high-pressure system that developed over the mainland coast that made progress against the fast-flowing Tasman current almost impossible. Apart from a close shave with an uncharted oil rig to the south of the island which he sighted close astern after *Leda* had sailed past, the tactic paid off, for thereafter he slowly overhauled his smaller rival to take the lead less than 20 miles from the finish.

For de Roux, of course, the voyage had been no less taxing. Apart from two knockdowns, he also had had to contend with ineffective self-steering, damaged rigging, a broken sat/nav and sextant, and a defunct diesel auxiliary which left him without any means of generating electricity. Despite all this, the Frenchman still managed to finish six days ahead of his nearest Class 2 rival.

Richard Broadhead, who had been out of radio contact for all but three days of the voyage, was the next to follow. *Perseverance* crossed the line on 2 January in a very sorry state. Looking at her broken pulpit, damaged mast and its loose rigging, a wardrobe of torn and tattered sails, and her broken self-steering gear, it was not difficult to appreciate the traumas this Englishman had gone through during the previous two months.

Her condition was in stark contrast to the Fast Passage 39

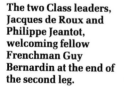

The two Class leaders, Jacques de Roux and Philippe Jeantot, welcoming fellow Frenchman Guy Bernardin at the end of the second leg.

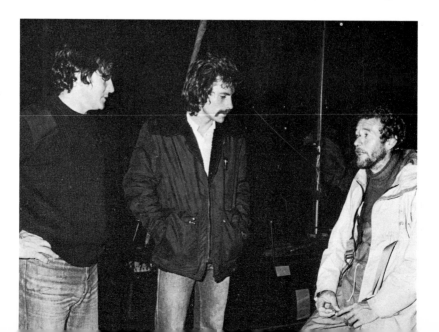

production cruiser *Mooneshine*, which brought Francis Stokes and his 'cabin boy' in to a hero's welcome two days later. Apart from suffering a number of failed breakaway couplings to her Aries self-steering, the yacht and her crew had survived their ordeal virtually unscathed and the yacht looked ready to continue on to Cape Horn just as she was.

Four hours later, the two Americans were joined in their celebrations by Guy Bernardin and his now battered *Ratso II* which, considering her size, did well to finish a day ahead of Yukoh Tada's larger *Koden Okera V* and three days ahead of Richard McBride's *City of Dunedin*.

After the salutary lessons learned during the first hours of this leg, Dan Byrne chose an extreme northerly route across the Indian Ocean to avoid the worst of the storms, but then ran close to adding a third statistic to the race when sleep overtook him on the home stretch towards Sydney:

Jan 5: 38-59S, 146-57E

The worst scare of the voyage today. I'd been up since 4 am guiding *Fantasy* through the Bass Strait and its islands, reefs and rocks. At nightfall, I approached and then threaded my way through several offshore oil-drilling rigs. At 9 pm I was lining up my course to pass one drilling platform, lighted like a Christmas tree. It was about 12 miles dead ahead, so I decided to take a thirty-minute nap. I set my kitchen timer – and awoke four hours later. The oil rig was nowhere in sight. I don't know whether I passed to the left or right, or how close. I had no inkling I was that tired. This was exactly the type of circumstance that put *Gipsy Moth* on the rocks at Gabo Island, 60 miles ahead.

The former newspaper editor completed the course a day later, to take tenth place overall, seven days ahead of the tailender Richard Konkolski, who reached Sydney the day after the fleet had departed.

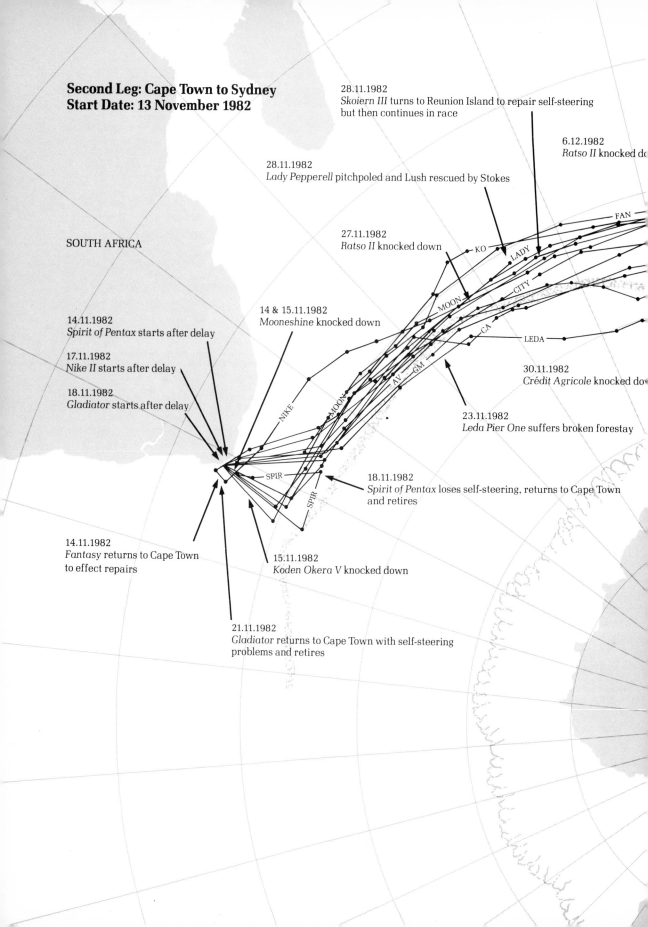

Second Leg: Cape Town to Sydney
Start Date: 13 November 1982

SOUTH AFRICA

28.11.1982
Skoiern III turns to Reunion Island to repair self-steering but then continues in race

6.12.1982
Ratso II knocked d

28.11.1982
Lady Pepperell pitchpoled and Lush rescued by Stokes

27.11.1982
Ratso II knocked down

14.11.1982
Spirit of Pentax starts after delay

17.11.1982
Nike II starts after delay

18.11.1982
Gladiator starts after delay

14 & 15.11.1982
Mooneshine knocked down

30.11.1982
Crédit Agricole knocked do

23.11.1982
Leda Pier One suffers broken forestay

18.11.1982
Spirit of Pentax loses self-steering, returns to Cape Town and retires

14.11.1982
Fantasy returns to Cape Town to effect repairs

15.11.1982
Koden Okera V knocked down

21.11.1982
Gladiator returns to Cape Town with self-steering problems and retires

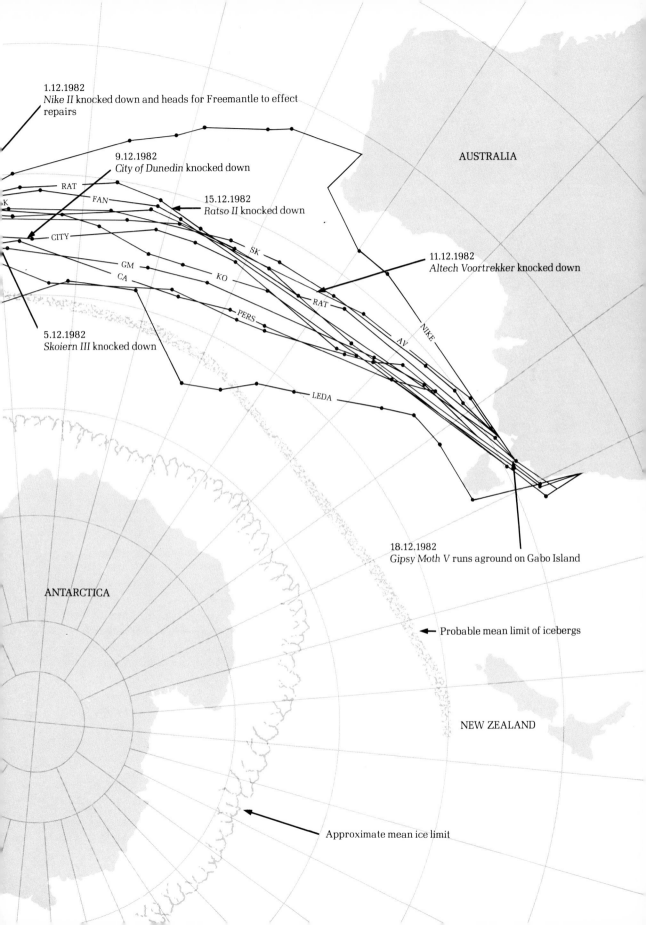

1.12.1982
Nike II knocked down and heads for Freemantle to effect repairs

9.12.1982
City of Dunedin knocked down

15.12.1982
Ratso II knocked down

11.12.1982
Altech Voortrekker knocked down

5.12.1982
Skoiern III knocked down

18.12.1982
Gipsy Moth V runs aground on Gabo Island

AUSTRALIA

ANTARCTICA

NEW ZEALAND

RAT

FAN

CITY

GM

CA

SK

KO

RAT

PERS

LEDA

AV

NIKE

K

← Probable mean limit of icebergs

← Approximate mean ice limit

Third Leg:
Sydney to Rio de Janeiro

The remarkable lead of eight days and ten hours that Philippe Jeantot now held over the fleet at the half-way stage of the race overshadowed to a large extent the equally outstanding performance of his fellow Frenchman Jacques de Roux. Unlike the race leader, who had experienced a relatively easy passage through the Southern Ocean, he was almost forced to retire on *Skoiern* because of self-steering problems, and also suffered two major knockdowns, yet he still managed to widen his lead to eight days and five hours over his nearest Class 2 rivals.

To many commentators at this Australian port both of these leads now looked unassailable. With so much time in hand, they reasoned, the two had only to cruise the remaining 11,000 miles back to the Newport finish line to secure a unique French double. Those behind them on elapsed time would have to push their yachts well beyond the limits of safety right across the world's most inhospitable ocean to Cape Horn to stand any chance of catching up. But 'there's many a slip 'twixt cup and lip', and the next leg was to produce more than its share of upsets.

No one had escaped completely unscathed on the second leg, and most competitors had a great deal to do to prepare themselves and their yachts to meet the 16 January deadline for the start of the 8250-mile third leg to Rio de Janeiro. For some, funds were now running desperately low, particularly in Neville Gosson's case for he had first to fend off creditors keen to take possession of his boat, then find the wherewithal to make good all the damage sustained to *Leda's* sails and rigging. While suppliers to his building company may not have been welcomed at Pier One with open arms, friends keen to help certainly were. A ready band of helpers worked to replace *Leda's* broken stays and chafed running rigging, and businessman Jack Rooklyn provided the local Australian entrant with sails salvaged from his yacht *Apollo*, wrecked off the Australian coast three years earlier. In fact, by the time he left, Gosson drew so much support that *Leda Pier One* was better prepared than at any other time in the race.

Jacques de Roux and Guy Bernardin attracted support from another unexpected quarter – the Banque Nationale de Paris. Doubtless stung by the rich publicity harvested in France from Philippe Jeantot's performance by its rival business house Crédit Agricole, the bank decided to generate a little of its own by sponsoring the two other Frenchmen for the remainder of the voyage. The security of having a bank behind them provided obvious benefits, but it did not insulate the two from all their problems. On the eve of the start De Roux was still waiting anxiously for delivery

 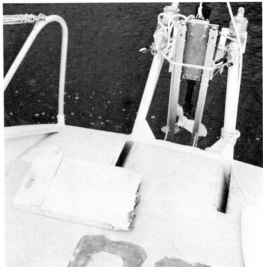

of a new sat/nav unit, because the man who came to replace the original, lost from *Skoiern's* masthead during one of her second leg knockdowns, dropped the first replacement unit overboard as he was transferring it from the dockside at Pier One. For his part Bernardin discovered to his dismay at the last minute that his steering had been rigged improperly, a problem that eventually led to a delay in his departure.

On *Crédit Agricole*, Jeantot was busy overseeing repairs to his mast and attending to broken stanchions and toe rail damaged during his knockdown off the Kerguelen Islands, as well as organizing a replacement for the wooden daggerboard that had snapped at some point during the voyage from Cape Town. Improved self-steering systems headed the work lists drawn up by skippers Reed, Broadhead and Tada. Bertie Reed had an Atom wind-vane self-steering system airfreighted to Sydney, but Broadhead and Tada, noting the success Neville Gosson had enjoyed since the start with his locally made Flemming equipment, chose to instal similar units on their yachts.

Richard McBride, who had just eight days in port before the re-start, was faced with hauling his yacht out of the water, installing a new generator, repairing his self-steering, storing food and replacing the running rigging on *City of Dunedin*, and though he had a helper in fellow-countryman Bede Beaumont, who travelled ahead to each of the pit-stops to lend a hand, the work still left little time for him to recuperate. This was also true for Dan Byrne, who had to instal an alternator and replace some of the solar panels which now showed signs of water penetration. He was also waiting anxiously for an electrician who could check *Fantasy's* wiring to ensure that the problems faced after leaving Cape Town did not recur in the Tasman.

Left: Yukoh Tada showing the makeshift repair to his spinnaker pole after the spar broke during the voyage through the Southern Ocean from Cape Town.

Right: The starboard daggerboard of *Crédit Agricole*, which was snapped in two on the voyage between Cape Town and Sydney. The damage sustained underlines the extreme pressures rudders and self-steering equipment are subjected to in the conditions of the Southern Ocean.

Crédit Agricole **taking a clear lead as the fleet sails through Sydney Heads at the beginning of the leg round Cape Horn to Rio de Janeiro.**

For some, Sunday, 16 January came all too soon, but Pier One was jam-packed on the day, with the vast crowd giving each of the skippers a rousing send-off as they set out once more to battle with the elements. Out in the harbour there was even more congestion, the chaos rivalling the start of the annual Sydney/Hobart classic each Boxing Day. An estimated 1000 spectator craft carried those keen to take a last look at these masochistic soloists and thousands more lined the cliffs round to Sydney Heads. Most skippers looked relaxed, enjoying this unaccustomed stardom to the full. They were more than half way now, had tasted the Southern Ocean and come to terms with its ferocity. From now on there would be no more turning back. Only the face of Guy Bernardin looked anxious and there was good reason. Just as he was preparing for the tow out the Frenchman discovered to his horror that *Ratso's* steering was still not rigged correctly and he was forced to wait impatiently as the others departed for the special tools required to strip the system down once more. By 3.00pm the fault had been rectified – or so he thought, but when he came to turn the wheel as *Ratso* took up her tow, he found the wires had now been rigged up in reverse, so the whole system had to be stripped down yet again, delaying his departure until much later in the day. In fact, the start had had to be delayed for an hour anyway to allow the nine other competitors to reach the start area through waters heavily cut up by the ferry boat race that preceded the BOC event. When the gun was eventually fired at 3.00pm, marking the high point of Sydney's water festival, all got away to clear start – well, almost. *Fantasy*, *Leda Pier One* and *Crédit Agricole* led the way through the wake of the spectator fleet, but Richard Broadhead, misjudging the distance mark, caught a line round *Perseverance's* self-steering gear and lost valuable time cutting it loose.

Bertie Reed's *Altech Voortrekker* suffered continual problems with her self-steering. In Sydney the South African replaced the Aries wind-vane gear with Atom equipment but this did not solve all his problems. The yacht was also equipped with a Plastimo electronic auto-pilot linked to the tiller but this was worked beyond its capacity and eventually burnt out.

If the warmth of the Australian summer and the spectacular farewell as Jeantot led the fleet out to sea lulled any into a false sense of well-being, the sudden change in the conditions experienced during that first week at sea quickly brought the ten sailors back to reality. The Tasman can be an uncomfortable sea at the best of times, but the southerly head winds that now prevailed kicked up the waves into a chop that soon began to tell on skippers and equipment. Richard McBride suffered a severe migraine attack almost immediately after the start, which wasn't helped when he found that he also had to contend with inoperative self-steering and a faulty log, both of which he thought had been repaired in Sydney. Neville Gosson was also unwell, a bad dose of 'mal de mer' keeping him in his bunk for much of the time during the first few days at sea. On *Voortrekker*, Bertie Reed was pleased to find his Atom self-steering could handle the strong headwinds satisfactorily, but was less than happy when the hydraulic backstay adjustor failed soon after the start. It was an uncomfortable time for all, described best by Dan Byrne in his diary:

> The Tasman Sea is a tough body of water. Short, nasty chop. *Fantasy* bangs along, tripping on waves and jolting almost to a stop before she finds her way again. The bow scoops water up and back over the boat. I've never seen that happen before. Waves over the bow, yes, but not the boat plunging and digging her bow in the short, steep waves.

As Richard Konkolski prepared to leave Sydney seven days behind the fleet in his 13.41-m (44-ft) yacht, now renamed *Nike III*, Philippe Jeantot was already nearing Bounty Island off the south-eastern tip of New Zealand, having covered more than 1300 miles in that first week. Astern of him by about 90 miles was Bertie Reed, who held a similar sized lead over Jacques de Roux, the Class 2 leader, and Richard Broadhead, who thought at one point during the week that he would have to divert to New Zealand to repair his rigging. The clevis pin securing the forestay at *Perseverance's* bow had lost its locking split pin, pulled half-way out of its toggle then bent under the strain, but after seeking advice over the ham radio waves from England, he decided the pin, now back in place and resecured, would probably hold so long as he kept an eye on it. The fifth and sixth yachts, *Koden Okera V* and *Leda Pier One*, had already dropped 300 miles astern of *Crédit Agricole* at this stage, and were followed by *Mooneshine*, *City of Dunedin* and *Fantasy*. The odd man out was Guy Bernardin who, having started late, decided to take a flyer round New Zealand's northern cape rather than follow the others on their shorter course south.

'Having the smallest boat I felt I had to take a different course to the others in order to beat them,' he explained to me in Rio. It was quite a gamble, for though the reaching winds he enjoyed that week helped *Ratso* to stay with the leaders easterly, the Frenchman still had to drop south in order to round Cape Horn, where he was expected to lose out badly.

By now Neville Gosson had recovered his sea legs but Richard McBride's migraine attack had not diminished. After finding the pills he carried to quell his headache had migrated to the bilges, he arranged a rendezvous off Stewart Island to collect more medication as well as a replacement log. He was eventually met off the island's south-western point by the fishing boat *Arun*, which towed him into Broad Bay where a helicopter dropped the stores to him early the following morning. The diversion should have put him at the back of the fleet but with *Fantasy* becalmed that day, the two remained almost level as if set on a private race across the Pacific.

Up ahead, Bertie Reed was holding Jeantot's lead to a narrow 90 mile margin, having covered altogether 478 miles during the previous three days, and was now confidently anticipating reaching the Horn by 20 February in 24 days' time. In fact he made it a day ahead of schedule, but as if to teach him not to look too far ahead, *Voortrekker* was knocked flat shortly after. 'What a mess down below', the South African wrote in his log after the 16-year-old yacht had recovered. 'A peanut butter jar breaks, eggs on the deck head, apples, oranges, butter etc. all mixed together. Had to reduce the mainsail to third reef. One can never have too much wind; it's the sea that wipes you out.'

The conditions were no better the next day either. He wrote:

Wind still from the south at 25–35 knots. Surfing up to 14 knots at times with triple reefed main and staysail. The odd wave still breaks on top of us trying to put us on our side. Had a few close calls. Barometer has been dropping steadily. Not all that comfortable.

The last remark was typical understatement. In the end the conditions proved too much for *Voortrekker's* Atom self-steering which left the South African with no alternative but revert to his

In contrast to the rest of the fleet, Guy Bernardin took a course to the north of New Zealand in the hope of avoiding the heavy conditions that came close to overwhelming his small yacht on the previous leg.

electronic autopilot until he could repair the vane system. Two hours later the radio also went on the blink but not before he had got a position through to Richard Broadhead some 100 miles astern, who was having an equally rough ride. His Flemming self-steering was standing up well, though the constant chafe in the lines where they passed through the steering arm block meant that he had to replace the rope every seven or eight hours. He had other problems too, for *Perseverance* continued to leak badly and as the winds built up to force 9 at the end of that second week, much of the water breaking across the deck found its way below to fill the bilges every twelve hours.

The yacht was taking a really thorough battering, and several times she crashed down from a wave crest into the trough below with such a bone-jarring force that the shock spewed all the contents from the lockers across the cabin sole. The only element of comedy was when Broadhead's alarm clock, which steadfastly refused to ring throughout the voyage, for once fulfilled its intended function when breaking loose in the heavy seas and falling on the sleeping Englishman as he lay in his bunk.

A general view of *Crédit Agricole's* deck, showing how all the sheets and control lines led aft to the control pit. In adverse conditions a water-tight door could close off the companionway.

The stationary low creating these high winds was to have a profound effect on the race, for in blocking the yachts' easterly track it scattered the fleet north and south. Reed and Broadhead, now less than 50 miles apart, chose to head north in search of more favourable winds, while Jeantot chose the opposite course. It was soon evident which was the better move, for despite suffering a knockdown which left *Crédit Agricole* with a torn mainsail and damaged rudder, the Frenchman increased his lead by a further 120 miles over his South African rival who was 400 miles further north by the end of the weekend. 'I knew we were too far over when all the things inside the cabin landed broken upside down', he said of his violent capsize on arrival in Rio at the end of this leg, adding somewhat ruefully: 'and my head was the first to meet the side of the boat!'

It was another two days before the weather moderated sufficiently for Jeantot to dive over the side and inspect the damage to the rudder, when he found to his dismay that the bottom bearing linking rudder to skeg had torn loose. After describing the problem over the radio to designer Guy Ribadeau Dumas in France, *Crédit Agricole's* designer advised him to keep speed below 15 knots, saying that if he let it climb up to 20 knots the foil was likely to break. The task that was to prove much easier said than done in the high rolling swells that prevailed.

Further astern, Jacques de Roux had also chosen to head south, a move that rewarded him with an important 200-mile lead over Neville Gosson's *Leda Pier One*, who in turn now held a small 30-mile advantage in sailing distance to the Horn over Yukoh Tada, now nicknamed the 'Iceman' on the inter-yacht radio net after taking a flyer well to the south of the fleet. This shorter great circle course, which eventually took the Japanese sailor close to 62°, well inside the ice limit, reduced the distance he had to sail over competitors tracking 10° to the north, including Francis Stokes, by almost a quarter. The American, who already trailed the Tokyo taxi driver, Tada, by 180 miles however, held a similar great circle advantage over Guy Bernardin, who must by now have regretted his flyer round the north of New Zealand. Quite apart from the extra distance this had added, his northerly position had still not insulated him from bad weather and the Frenchman was finding *Ratso* continuing to broach uncontrollably in the force 8/9 gale that developed at the start of that third week, despite the 225 kg (500 lb) of sand he had stowed under her cabin sole in Sydney to increase ballast.

Bernardin may have been cursing the conditions, but at least the winds were from astern, while the others were all battling against an easterly storm. Neville Gosson wrote in his log at the end of his 18th day at sea:

> What a lousy day it is. Cold and miserable with a force 7 to 8 right on the nose again. The seas are up and the boat is jumping all over the place. Not conducive to pleasant sailing. I would prefer to be in a nice restaurant with a bottle of red and good company. As it was not to be I helped myself to the Scotch instead. I am sick of constant easterlies in this so-called westerly dominated area.

These head winds, which remained for much of the next week continued to favour those to the south. By the following weekend Philippe Jeantot had increased his lead to 500 miles over Jacques de Roux, who in moving up to second overall had been 200 miles nearer to the Horn than Reed at one time during the week, until the South African finally benefited from following winds to the north and whittled this back down to a slim 10-mile margin. Close behind Reed, virtually the same distance from the Horn, was Richard Broadhead, who continued to shadow *Voortrekker's* Argos plots despite having to make running repairs to a broken spinnaker pole mast track that poked a hole through the mainsail, and hitting a mysterious object during the week.

He wrote of the incident in his log on that twenty-first day of the leg:

0500 GMT: Hit something in the water. Boat slows dramatically and bow dips. No sound of collision but it felt like running on to a sandbank. I think it was only the bottom of the keel which touched. Presume it was a whale but could not see anything in the water astern.

Further south by 10°, Yukoh Tada, still on his extreme course well inside the ice limit, was maintaining his lead over Neville Gosson's *Leda Pier One*, which suffered a blown mainsail during the course of the week and now lagged about 700 miles behind the French leader. Behind the Australian yacht by another 300 miles, Francis Stokes in *Mooneshine* had now opened up more than a day's lead over Richard McBride and Dan Byrne, who were having the race of their lives running neck and neck 3000 miles from the Horn. But *Mooneshine's* fast passage that week had not been without incident.

Stokes wrote at the end of that fourth week:

My first gale in this ocean. Seas built up very quickly after supper and I ran with storm jib all night. Wind speed hit 50 knots on my instruments. I was reluctant to go directly down-wind (SE) so left the wind a bit on the port quarter. That's asking for trouble and sure enough we were knocked flat causing a typical jumble in the cabin. No damage on deck except the Aries vane broken and dodger frames bent. It's odd but *Fantasy* and *City of Dunedin*, 200 miles behind missed this wind.

By this time Bernardin, now nearly 340 miles further from the Horn than McBride and Byrne, must still have been kicking himself for making the wrong course decision, for he was now being fast overhauled by Richard Konkolski further south, who had now reduced his seven-day deficit to three.

Dan Byrne's *Fantasy* carried her life raft on the cabin top aft of the mast, ready for easy release should the need arise.

Two days later the leading yachts, now half way between New Zealand and Cape Horn, received similar weather to *Mooneshine*, a storm that led to one of the most dramatic rescue stories in ocean racing history. First to succumb to the wild force 12 conditions was Neville Gosson, whose twenty-fifth day at sea is surely one that will remain forever etched on his mind. He told me later:

> I survived the day but I'm not sure how. The wind swung to the north during the night and blew force 8, then at daylight backed to the NW and increased to 96 km/h (60 mph) gusting 112 km/h (70 mph) until sunset. Surfing down one 12-m (40-ft) wave, we got barrelled by a northern cross swell which broke over and spun us like a top. It takes a lot to put this boat down because it is so beamy but she just screwed round sideways into the seas which then broke over pushing us right under. I had just gone down below to make a cup of coffee, having been up all night and much of the day before trying to keep the boat going. The kettle hadn't been on for two minutes when the wave hit. It was just as if someone had pulled a chair from under me. I must have flown 3 m (10 ft) through the air because I split my head on the bookshelf on the other side, smashing the woodwork, before being thrown back again and landing on my spine. The next thing I remember was waking up feeling very sore and finding the kettle dribbling warm water all over me!

When *Leda* finally righted herself the cabin was full of water. The Australian was cold, wet and barely able to move for the pain in his back, but the boat had to be bailed out and a check made for damage. When he finally struggled up through the companionway the scene on deck was like a jigsaw with lines and equipment strewn everywhere. Worse still, the force of the knockdown had pulled the starboard chainplate anchoring the shrouds to the deck away from its supporting frames welded to the hull. Fate had struck the luckless Australian once again, and for the third leg running he had no alternative but to limp on under reduced sail and hope that the damage would not get worse.

The same night, Reed, Broadhead and de Roux, unaware of Gosson's troubles, each reported a similar storm during their usual daily radio link. Though neither Reed nor Broadhead mentioned it, both sensed from the tone of Jacques de Roux that he was worried. *Skoiern's* anemometer, he told them, had rarely been registering less than 55 knots and he said she had been taking in a lot of water for the past couple of days. Before signing off, each agreed to link up an hour earlier the next day. When the time came and Jacques' voice was not heard the other two could only wonder if something had happened.

It certainly had: *Skoiern* had been pitchpoled by a huge following sea. It all happened within seconds. The Frenchman, lying in his quarter berth, felt the boat roll through 180° – and then stay there. Water poured in so fast that the change in pressure made his

ears pop, and as he desperately fought for air, crouching in darkness on the deck head, his sub-mariner's instinct told him the boat must be going straight down. Thank God she wasn't, but when she finally righted herself it was obvious that neither sailor nor yacht could carry on.

Poor de Roux, already suffering from exhaustion after a lengthy spell at the helm trying to keep *Skoiern* on an even keel, was now wet through, bleeding, bruised and half-concussed. His yacht was without a mast, her forward deck hatch had been ripped away and, while she floated with little more than 10 cm (4 in) of air space under her deck, each successive wave deposited more water below decks. It was a question of survival, and after tripping the panic switch on his Argos transponder, he started pumping ... hoping someone would get to him before it was too late.

It took two hours and three minutes for de Roux's distress signal to reach the Argos decoding station at Toulouse in France. The race organisers in Newport were immediately alerted and given the Frenchman's position as 55° 29'S 126° 55'W. It was deduced from later signals that he was drifting in an easterly direction at a little under 1½ knots. Was *Skoiern* merely disabled, or was de Roux in his life raft already, having taken the portable transponder with him? Race control had no way of knowing. What they did know however, was that with no shipping in the area and the nearest land 1800 miles away, the only immediate help to hand was from other competitors in the race.

Nearest was Neville Gosson, 165 miles north-west of the Frenchman, followed by Richard Broadhead, almost twice that distance away to the north-east, and it was left to Newport ham Rob Koziomkowski, to alert his worldwide network of fellow enthusiasts to help in contacting them. Gosson was the first to have a scheduled radio contact with a ham in Australia, but having worked through the day to get *Leda* shipshape after her roll, he took two pain-killing tablets and slept through the alarm, missing the vital message by 15 minutes.

It was twelve long hours before any contact was finally made. Ham enthusiast Matt Johnstone, living in the sleepy town of Owaka situated on New Zealand's South Island, who had been monitoring the airwaves since being alerted by Koziomkowski, suddenly picked up Broadhead transmitting Bertie Reed's position to another ham and interrupted their transmission. On hearing the news, the Englishman agreed to help immediately, but within five minutes of turning back into those mountainous Southern Ocean swells he knew he was attempting a feat that, as one newspaper was to put it, was to be several times more difficult than finding a needle in a haystack. The biggest worry was that with the weather moderating, *Perseverance*, which had no means of auxiliary propulsion, her propeller having been removed before the race to reduce drag, was unable to manage more than five knots under sail. At that rate it

Richard Broadhead's rescue of Jacques de Roux would not have been possible without the Argos Satellite automatic position reporting system. Transmission by ham operators of the information it supplied pinpointed *Skoiern III*'s changing positions during de Roux's 60-hour ordeal.

would take Broadhead at least forty hours to get back to de Roux's position. Would he be too late?

It took the exhausted de Roux 3½ hours to pump the water out of *Skoiern's* hull but she continued to ship a lot of water through the open hatch, and a second hole punched through the hull as de Roux was cutting away the broken rigging. His mistake had been to cut the shrouds before the halyards with the result that one section of the broken spar had swung out like a pendulum and made the fatal hole through the alloy plating. Though the rest of the world could only guess, he himself knew his situation was critical and he was now pumping almost continuously.

Johnstone and Koziomkowski worked as a team to feed Broadhead every hour over the radio with the latest position reports for both his own yacht and Skoiern, sometimes passing the information via a ham in Tahiti when propagation became too bad for them to broadcast clearly. The only problem for Broadhead was that some of these satellite fixes were interspersed with dead reckoned plots, and with nothing to differentiate between the two the confusion over his own position eventually led him to ignore some of the information and plot his own course towards the stricken yachtsman.

At 11.00 GMT the next day, *Perseverance* was thought to be 20 miles South-east of *Leda Pier One* and as no one had yet managed to raise Gosson, Broadhead fired off a red parachute flare in the hope that this might attract his attention, but there was no response. In fact another twelve hours passed by before Gosson was finally alerted by his ham contact in Australia, and though he also joined in the search, main hopes were now pinned on Broadhead who by now was much nearer the Frenchman.

Broadhead finally reached de Roux's reported position area at 1.00 GMT (05.00 local time) on the Friday 11 February, forty-seven hours after being alerted, but saw nothing of *Skoiern* or her skipper. Thankfully the fog that had shrouded *Perseverance* for much of this rescue mission had now lifted but the grey skies and rolling seas pushed by the force 5 nor'wester hindered visibility, though at least there was another twelve hours of light in which to continue the search. He waited for the next set of Argos position reports from Matt Johnstone, in the hope of following de Roux's tack. For an hour he saw nothing and began to doubt now whether the Frenchman could have survived three days in these freezing conditions.

Thinking he must have overstood, Broadhead went below to discuss his next move with Matt over the radio and as they talked de Roux suddenly sighted *Perseverance* 45 m (50 yards) away.

Filled with elation, the Frenchman jumped up and down on *Skoiern*'s deck, shouting and waving for all he was worth, delighted

Jacques de Roux (left), who was rescued from the pitchpoled *Skoiern III* by Richard Broadhead (right), on *Perseverance of Medina*.

to have rescue finally in sight. But elation turned to despair when his calls went unheard and the British yacht, her deck deserted, sailed on into the distance. De Roux grabbed a red flare and set it off, then another and another until the seven he carried had all been spent, but not one brought any response from *Perseverance*.

Broadhead finally came back on deck shortly before 20.00 GMT, having made himself a cup of tea. Searching the horizon his eyes suddenly caught a flash of white about 2 miles in the distance. At first he thought it was an iceberg, then the bridge of a ship and thanked God someone else was there to help in the search. Then, as a wave lifted *Skoiern* clear he realized it was the sail of her jury rig. 'I've found him, I've found him,' Broadhead yelled excitedly down the microphone to Matt, after rushing back down to the radio set.

As he turned back towards the stricken yacht, sailing towards him at 3 knots, wind and seas were beginning to build up. There was no time to waste. Bringing the two yachts alongside in the uneven swell called for the very best seamanship and, not surprisingly perhaps, the two yachts collided several times before de Roux finally abandoned his yacht on the fourth pass. During the second and third passes, the Frenchman threw his belongings over, then prepared himself for the leap across as Broadhead lined *Perseverance's* bows up for a fourth time.

'Jump ... now', Broadhead shouted as the two yachts drew alongside. But Jacques hesitated before leaping across the gap and in that split second, a wave thrust the two yachts further apart. Instead of landing safely on *Perseverance's* deck, he fell short outside the lifelines. 'He was absolutely knackered', Broadhead said when recounting the story later. 'He just hung there by his armpits over the top of the lifelines and if the two boats had come together again, he would have lost his legs. I rushed forward from the cockpit and grabbing him by the seat of his pants, pulled him onboard. He then just lay there on deck talking non-stop for five minutes or more and in the end I had to stop him by pointing out I had to go back to the wheel and steer the boat!'

The rescue had been made just in time for shortly after, the winds were gusting up to 35 knots and four hours later *Skoiern's* Argos transponder stopped transmitting, indicating that the yacht had finally sunk, making her the third to be lost in this race. By now, though, both had their heads down for a well-earned rest as *Perseverance* headed at once towards the Horn.

Three days later the British yacht made a rendezvous with the French frigate *Henry*, which had been despatched from Gambia Island nearly 2000 miles to the north soon after the emergency began, and the submarine commander was transferred by Zodiac in exchange for a generous hamper of food and wine as a special 'thank you' to Broadhead from the French Navy. 'A lot of it was just good luck', Broadhead admitted modestly a month later, after his arrival at the third stopover port. 'We were very lucky that the fog cleared away and the weather held just long enough for me to find him.' He also praised the Argos tracking system and de Roux's seamanship in keeping his yacht afloat until help arrived. 'I would never had found him if he had taken to his life raft. I just wouldn't have seen it in those seas,' the Englishman explained.

Two days later, Philippe Jeantot, now more than 500 miles ahead of second-placed Bertie Reed finally reached Cape Horn. Like everyone else, he had read that the weather around this rocky

The leaders, including Bertie Reed on *Altech Voortrekker*, set spinnakers whenever possible and kept them up even at night or while they slept, relying on self-steering equipment to control their yachts.

outpost, marking the divide between the grey-green waters of the Southern Ocean and the brown of the Atlantic, was almost always bad, blowing a full gale most days, a storm the rest, building up to hurricane strength for short periods every three months.

Though robbed of a sighting by darkness, the experience left Jeantot far from disappointed for the conditions were just as he had imagined. Rounding in a 50-knot westerly at 03.00 GMT on 16 February *Crédit Agricole* sped into the record books, setting a new single-handed record from Sydney of 29 days 23 hours, beating the previous best time set in 1974 by Alain Colas aboard his trimaran *Manureva* (ex *Pen Duick IV*) by a massive six-day margin. In doing so the Flying Frenchman also set a fastest seven-day run by any single-handed circumnavigator of 1552 miles during that week, but a best 24-hour run of 246 miles – an average of 10.7 knots – set on 10 February was one mile short of a new record set, sixteen days later by the chasing Class 2 yacht *Nike III*, more than 1000 miles astern and now on level terms with *Ratso II*, Guy Bernardin's yacht.

When Bertie Reed arrived off this notorious Cape three days later, however, conditions could not have contrasted more with the picture painted in the South African's mind. Instead of towering seas, white water and leaden, wind-filled skies, a gentle 10-knot breeze made it all seem like a Saturday afternoon sail. Indeed, so calm were the conditions that he anchored off the island of Deceit to take up an offer from the Chilean escort ship there to greet the competitors, and to replenish his fresh water supplies, spilt during the knockdown two weeks before. 'A great bunch of guys', Reed wrote in his log, 'and it's a pity I could not spend more time at anchor, as the Horn is a beautiful sight.'

Next to round in the early hours of 23 February was the new Class 2 leader, Yukoh Tada. He had wanted to capture this stark white-capped landscape on video but was defeated by a combination of darkness and bad weather which forced him to stay 60 miles off. It was the same too for Neville Gosson, the next to arrive at midnight at the start of his forty-first day at sea. He wrote in his log:

> Well, here is one legend that lived up to its reputation. What a night trying to get around. It blew force 8 then 10 and the seas crashed all over us. We had only a staysail up and even that couldn't stand the rolling and jumping and wind, and out came the clew. The furled headsail came partly unfurled in the centre and what a job to try and unfurl it. It took two hours on a foredeck that was everywhere. I will never forget the Horn. It was so cold I was chilled to the bone and could not find a dry garment.

For Richard Broadhead, who drew abeam of the Horn little more than an hour later, conditions, of course, were just as bad, but it was not until the next morning that things finally got out of hand for the Englishman. A storm warning beforehand, advising of a 30–50 knot south-wester, was, he thought, no reason to alter course away. It was after all the Horn that he had sailed half way round the world to see. But like so many forecasts it was wrong, and a vicious 60-knot sou'wester built up as *Perseverance* approached. So steep were the seas that even the Chilean naval escort was driven to seek shelter behind one of the islands and Broadhead was left to beat round the infamous Cape alone under storm staysail and fully reefed main. The winds freed the following morning but this only confused the seas further and as he headed towards the Berwood Bank through steep standing waves, the Englishman knew it was only a question of time before disaster would strike. He recalled in Rio:

> I was hand steering but with the waves breaking either side. I knew I would be knocked over sooner or later. Eventually, I reconnected the Flemming self-steering and as it seemed to be handling the conditions as well as I could, I went below to bail the boat out. No sooner had I got on my hands and knees though, than the boat went over with such incredible force everything was thrown on to the starboard side. The Sailormat and Aries (self-steering) all broke adrift and smashed the woodwork. Bits of boom section, the liferaft, flares and a paraffin can all landed on my bunk just where my head would have been if I had been lying there and water poured through the hatch.

Opposite, top: *Altech Voortrekker* dropped anchor soon after rounding Cape Horn to replenish freshwater supplies lost during a knock down two weeks before. Conditions were like those on a Saturday-afternoon sail as supplies were taken in from the Chilean escort ship.

On deck he found the windward spinnaker pole had been wrenched from its attachment outside of the shrouds and now rested on a halyard winch on the mast. The spray hood protecting the main hatch had been ripped off and hung limply from the pulpit. He also found that the small plywood Flemming self-steering vane had snapped in two and guessed that *Perseverance* must have rounded up before being knocked over through 120° by a standing wave. Backing the staysail so that she would lie hove-to, Broadhead then went below again to bail the boat out and tidy up the mess but he had to contend with damp bedding until reaching Rio.

When Francis Stokes neared the Cape three days later on 27 February the winds had subsided but nevertheless he still had a surprise in store, as his log for that day tells:

A long day, but ultimately the most rewarding of the voyage – or even my life. Visibility one mile or less all day with fog, rain and snow. With no sun for two days and the sat/nav taking the whole weekend off, I was keeping a dead reckoning track with Diego

Francis Stokes's *Mooneshine*, now challenging strongly for Class 2 honours, rounded Cape Horn in sixth place just 12 miles ahead of Richard Konkolski's *Nike III*. Dan Byrne's *Fantasy* reached this landmark on the same day.

Opposite, bottom: For Guy Bernardin on *Ratso II* the sight of Cape Horn was 'one of the Seven Wonders of the World.'

Right: Unlike most of the entries, *Fantasy*, Dan Byrne's Valiant 40 production cruiser, was untroubled by self-steering problems, relying on an Aries wind-vane system, backed up by an electronic auto-pilot connected to the wheel.

Below: HMS *Exeter*, the British warship that escorted the yachts as they passed the Falkland Islands, photographed from Dan Byrne's *Fantasy*.

Left: The self-steering vane on *City of Dunedin* only worked satisfactorily in strong conditions.

Below: *City of Dunedin* in wild conditions in the Southern Ocean.

City of Dunedin, which ran aground on East Falkland, arrived in Rio 12 days after the rest of the fleet had set off on the last leg.

Inset: Philippe Jeantot, the first to arrive off Rio, was dogged by light airs at the end of the third leg.

Right: Yukoh Tada posing for a photograph on one of the few occasions he held the tiller during the 27,000-mile race. 'Me velly lazy sailor, always rely on self-steering,' he would say with a grin.

Below: The perspex dodger on *Altech Voortrekker* provided Bertie Reed with some protection when he stepped out through the main companionway hatch, particularly in the wild conditions of the Southern Ocean.

Right: *Nike III* leading *Crédit Agricole* soon after the start of the fourth leg.

Below: The perspex dome fitted on *Ratso II*, designed to allow Guy Bernardin to look out from the safety of his cabin, in practice misted up quickly, restricting his vision.

Ramirez, the intended landfall. At daylight, I set a course of 50°M aiming for the islands. After three hours and no improvement in visibility it seemed wise to bear off and go south. All this time the depth sounder refused to find bottom though I thought it should easily pick up the bank there. After four hours I turned NE again towards Cape Horn with the object of gaining the lee of Tierra del Fuego. With the change in conditions I had no thought of actually sighting anything. I was totally surprised then when the mists parted at 21.45 GMT (16.45 Local) and there I was 5 miles due south of Cape Horn – close enough to see details of the rocks. I don't know whether excitement or confusion was the greater. I was 20 miles ahead of my dead reckoning and found it hard to believe I was there.

Mooneshine rounded some 12 miles ahead of Richard Konkolski's *Nike III*, which had made quite remarkable progress since leaving Sydney and now led Class 2 on elapsed time for this leg after making a fine string of seven 200 miles plus daily runs. It had not all been plain sailing, though, and the Czech was perhaps lucky to make it at all. The exhaust pipe on the air-cooled generator fitted as a temporary measure in Sydney kept breaking loose during the voyage, filling the cabin with lethal fumes. He had taken the precaution of fitting an alarm but one night he forgot to switch it on and was nearly gassed as he lay in his bunk. Hearing the engine beat falter and thinking the fuel was about to run out, he switched on the lights to find the cabin engulfed in black smoke, and was overcome as he rushed to open the ports. 'The next thing I knew I woke up lying on the galley floor and just managed to pull myself out on deck to get fresh air', he told us in Rio; but though the experience gave him a severe headache for three days afterwards, it didn't slow him down. The Czech was robbed of his hoped-for sighting of the Cape, though, rounding the Horn in thick fog at 20.00 hours local time. Astern by 40 miles Richard McBride had better luck, calling over his radio the next morning as the mountain came into view: 'It's a major milestone in my life'.

He wrote in his log and diary:

All is black to the north but the great Cape can be felt in the particular quality of the sea and wind. A number of birds keep me company, storm petrels and prions dancing through the spray and foam, while a sooty albatross wheels overhead, sometimes riding the up-draft from my sails. Two dolphins appear almost alongside surfing on the face of a giant sea. Their presence fills me with joy and as I watch, my eye is drawn beyond the dark wall of cloud. And there, out of the murk, materializes the stark magnificence of Cape Horn! Massive – magnificent through the mist about three to four miles to the nor'nor-east. If one wanted a day with all the soul of Cape Horn this is it – winds gusting to 50 knots, huge seas and gloomy. A civilian aircraft buzzed me just as I was doing a massive broach

Opposite: *City of Dunedin* **running home under spinnaker.**

– hope they enjoyed it. Patrol vessel also in sight – it's like King's bloody Cross!

Dan Byrne's *Fantasy*, trailing the New Zealander's yacht by 140 miles, rounded 10 miles to the south at the dead of night but nevertheless felt this was to be the final turning point in his adventure. 'Now *Fantasy* is on her way home', he wrote on 27 February.

The four solar panels fitted to Dan Byrne's *Fantasy* to help charge batteries were fixed rather vulnerably around the cockpit on brackets.

For Guy Bernardin, the last in the line-up, now trailing the American by 100 miles, Cape Horn provided the ultimate challenge. This was his second attempt at fulfilling this long nurtured ambition but it came perilously close to a nightmare just 15 miles from his goal.

A force 6/7 gale the previous day had left *Ratso* with a broken forestay and her young skipper near to exhaustion, and as the winds began to recede that night, he took the opportunity to snatch a few hours sleep before making the final approach to the Horn. As he lay there, *Ratso* started luffing up into wind and he sensed something was wrong. He told us later:

My boat was talking to me, but I had 300 reasons for not getting up. Eventually though, I couldn't stand it any longer and climbing up on deck to adjust the sails saw a huge wall of green all around. It gave me a shock, I can tell you. The boat had sailed into a bay on Cape West and we were very close to the shore. I jumped up and tried to tack the boat but with only a heavily reefed mainsail and storm jib set, I had to put up more sail first.

A few hours later he rounded within half a mile of the Horn. 'It was a beautiful sight. The best of my life. It is one of the seven wonders of the world – and having seen it I will die quite happily', the young Frenchman enthused.

Most saw the Horn as the last major milestone in this BOC

The stresses to which Richard McBride's *City of Dunedin* were subjected around Cape Horn resulted in damage to the twin forestays and caused the skipper to alter course as the yacht neared the Falkland Islands.

Challenge, but any complacency that set in once compass headings showed north quickly evaporated when three days later radios buzzed with news of yet another catastrophe. Richard McBride had 'hit the bricks' on East Falkland just as Philippe Jeantot was nearing the finish.

Two days before, while on course towards the west of this disputed island group, the young New Zealander had taken advantage of a moderate spell in the weather to climb *City of Dunedin's* mainmast and repair one of her twin forestays, which had shown signs of fatigue before the Horn. Once at the top, however, he found that some strands had parted on the second stay as well. 'Bloody hell,' he wrote in his log, 'the core could already be cracked so I will have to make a repair on the first one.' The job of turning the one wire end-for-end and doubling the broken part through a heavy length of chain attached to the bow took all afternoon, and by the time he was finished, McBride was bruised and exhausted from his climb up the mast. He completed the job just in time, for that night the winds veered to the north and increased, to leave the yacht pounding heavily into the headseas. If he had not made the repair when he did one of the stays, if not both, would undoubtedly have snapped under the heavy strain and brought the mast down with them. But would his repair be strong enough?

McBride's concern was heightened when he heard over the radio that Konkolski had also suffered two broken forestays and was now seeking shelter from 40-knot headwinds among the islands to the north-west of this archipelago, and it was this that made him decide to run off to the east of the Falklands to lessen the strain on his own rig. Later, when discussing his move over the radio with Dan Byrne, the American warned him to keep a weather eye open for a shift in the wind that might put him on the rocks, in the same way that *Gipsy Moth* had been wrecked. But the warning was to no avail, for shortly after 23.00 hours on 1 March McBride sat down at his table with a cup of coffee, exhausted after an evening of continual sail changes – and promptly fell asleep. Two and a half hours later he was woken by a tremendous crash that shook the 12.80-m (42-ft) yacht from stem to stern. Byrne's worst fears had been realised. He wrote in his diary:

> As I wake and leap for the hatch, in one sickening instant, I know what has happened. While I have been taking an un-scheduled sleep, the wind has backed to the south, turning the boat north. My voyage has ended on the rocks somewhere on the south-east Falklands. Within a few seconds she is lying on her side against a ledge of solid rock, being pounded by a steady sou'wester. It is very dark, but occasionally enough moon shows through to show me that *City of Dunedin* is lying 50 m (55 yards) from a low rocky beach. The south-west swell is increasing and as I remove the sails the seas are sneaking over the boat and the noise is phenomenal.
>
> After securing equipment and sails I turn on the Argos alarm and after trying the marine frequencies without answer, I turn to the ever-watchful ham net. My mayday call is answered immediately by a station in Hawaii, but propagation is poor and over the next couple of hours – with failing batteries – I hear someone relay my position incorrectly and I have difficulty confirming my position.
>
> The boat quickly fills with water and I presume that the hull has been holed by the constant pounding. In between calls on the radio, I manage to walk ashore with a rope which I tie to a rock on the beach. Most likely we are on Bull Point, the south-eastern point of East Falkland. The night drags on, punctuated by short talks on the ham radio, and finally the moon comes out briefly and reveals my surroundings. We're on a beach running NW–SE, low land to the north-east and a couple of small islands to the south-east. The radio net has become world-wide and

eventually I speak to Race control in Newport, who have managed to obtain the latest Argos readings and a fix – I am on the mainland of East Falkland on Craigylea Point, part of Bull Point Peninsula.

Not long after daybreak I hear the welcome sound of an engine. A helicopter lands on the beach and shortly after I am transported to the efficient bustling world of a modern warship – HMS *Penelope*. I am treated with great kindness by the officers and enjoy a hot bath, breakfast and dry clothes and am later flown back to the boat, accompanied by the chief engineering officer and the bosun. With buckets and pumps we remove about 8 tonnes of water and find that the boat is not seriously holed – in fact the only hole is in the ballast keel and the water has come up through a pipe used to pour oil into the ballast. With the pipe sealed off no more water comes in.

Serving in the area under the command of the Royal Navy was Britain's largest ocean tug, *Salvageman*, and on hearing the news her master, Captain John Bolds, called the following day to offer help.

Unfortunately, the unnamed bay – later called Dick's Bay by locals – was uncharted and full of kelp weed, making the master

Hard aground. The sorry plight of *City of Dunedin*, which ran aground on Craigylea Point, East Falkland Island, on 1 March 1983 and was not refloated until 30 March.

The success of Philippe Jeantot can be attributed to seamanship of a high order and to the attention to detail that had been shown in the planning and construction of *Crédit Agricole.*

wary of positioning his ship close enough to tow the yacht off, so dashing initial hopes of an early rescue. A second attempt, two days later, this time with a launch from the survey ship HMS *Endurance* also failed, for by now the yacht had been driven well up the beach. Her recovery now required a major salvage operation, and another three weeks was to pass before anyone knew whether the schooner could be saved.

A day later, on 5 March, Philippe Jeantot finally crossed the Rio finish line at 02.59 GMT, after being slowed by light winds on the approach towards the Brazil coast. *Crédit Agricole's* damaged rudder, made worse by a second knockdown during a 50-knot gale the week before, had been his greatest worry, and with his two autopilots burnt out during the voyage and wind vane self-steering rendered useless in the light fickle winds that prevailed during the last stage of the voyage, he had been forced to steer by hand. 'The most difficult leg so far', was how the exhausted Frenchman described his voyage on arrival, but he still beat Bertie Reed by 51½ hours, increasing his overall lead to a commanding eleven days.

The South African Reed, plagued once more by self-steering troubles for most of the voyage, which he overcame at one point by cannibalizing a galley tap to repair the Atom, was followed six days later by Richard Broadhead, who had been slowed on the last stage of the voyage by a force 7 gale north of the Falklands which blew out his mainsail. The fantastic welcome he was given was made all the more poignant by the appearance of Jean Louis and Vera de Roux, Jacques' brother and his wife, who had flown in specially from Paris to provide a personal 'thank you' for his successful rescue.

They were still in town when news came through of yet another race drama, this one little more than 2 miles from the yacht club.

Yukoh Tada, caught in a driving rainstorm late that afternoon that cut visibility in the harbour to less than 50 m (55 yards), had run aground on the tiny island of Ilha da Laje – a low flat rock barely seen at high water, that acts as foundations for an old fort guarding the entrance to the inner harbour of this natural archipelago. After crossing the finish line off Copacabana Beach, the Japanese sailor had been instructed by the local race committee over the radio to

Opposite: Bertie Reed on
Altech Voortrekker at the
finish.

head towards the mouth of the harbour and wait for a towboat, but
unable to find the tow, even with his radar set, Tada kept going,
sailing at 6–7 knots under reefed mainsail – until running up on the
shallow rock close to the fort.

It was his cry over the VHF: 'On the locks! ... On the locks!' that
first alerted the reception committee to Tada's plight and led them to
the island, where they found the agitated skipper standing alongside
his stranded yacht. Initially, the military refused permission for
anyone to land and help the hapless sailor but in the two hours it
took to get the order rescinded, Philippe Jeantot and a group of
diving friends devised a plan to refloat the yacht. Holding *Okera*
down on her side with anchors and line attached to the masthead,
they then waited for the tide to rise before towing her clear. The
principal damage was to Tada's pride, for his yacht had escaped
with just a scrape along her port side, and drunk with relief once his
ordeal was over, the Class 2 overall leader said to each of his
rescuers, with obvious gratitude: 'I am velly lucky man. Tank you ...
Tank you.'

Three days later the early finishers were joined first by Neville
Gosson, who had been forced to take things easy after Cape Horn by
the widening split that developed across *Leda*'s deck where the
starboard chain plate had pulled away, then by Richard Konkolski,
Francis Stokes and Guy Bernardin. Konkolski's performance in
beating two Class I boats and all but one of his Class 2 rivals, despite
leaving Sydney seven days late, was an achievement that drew
respect and admiration from all. Though last to round Cape Horn,
the Frenchman managed to overhaul Dan Byrne during that storm off
the Falklands to finish 250 miles ahead of the irrepressible American, who joked on his arrival five days later: 'I decided to stay back
so that I could help any of the other guys ahead of me.'

Koden Okera V, co-
sponsored by a Japanese
electronics company, was
equipped with every
technical facility, from
colour radar to fish-
finding sonar. The radar
set, mounted on a
stainless steel platform
over the cockpit, did not
help him when caught in
a driving rainstorm off
Rio, when the yacht ran
aground on a small island
shortly after crossing the
finishing line.

Back on the Falklands, plans were being drawn up to refloat *City of Dunedin*, which by now had been driven so far up the beach by the southerly gales that the tide now barely reached her keel. To move the 15 tonnes yacht the 40 m (130 ft) into deep water was to become a major military operation involving a team of divers, the labour force from the nearby North Arm settlement and men from Z Company, First Royal Hampshire Regiment, equipped with a 5-tonne anchor borrowed from the Royal Fleet Auxiliary *Sir Tristram* and dropped by helicopter out in the bay, endless lengths of rope and wire, and three tractors.

The New Zealander wrote in his diary on 26 March as plans progressed to haul his yacht off the rocks on the tide:

Richard McBride spent six days in Rio undertaking repairs to *City of Dunedin* and revictualling before setting out on the last leg.

> My concern that I may be disqualified from the race by being over the 30-day limit is put to rest, which is a relief, and soon the anchor is placed by a huge Chinook helicopter and all the gear assembled. With block and tackle placed by Navy divers the tractors begin to pull and the boat moves easily towards the water. A strong sou'westerly is blowing but it can't be helped, we have to continue. Soon *City of Dunedin* is rising and falling to the swells but our problems are not yet over. The gear fails and the tractors are unable to pull any further. I spend a sleepless night as rudder and keel pound on the rocky sea floor. Early in the morning a shackle parts and the yacht ends up on her side on the rocks again. Fortunately, the weather improves rapidly this time and two days later we're afloat again (30 March). There is no wind at all this time so with the assistance of Commander John Webber, who has organised the salvage, and Charlie Smith from North Arm, we row the boat's own anchor out to the limit of its warp with the dinghy and warp her out to it. This is done at least eight times so that by evening, we are almost on the edge of the kelp, over half a mile from the beach and no matter which direction the wind comes from I can now sail clear.

Opposite, top: Yukoh Tada, winner of Class 2, celebrating his success.

The damage to *City of Dunedin* was surprisingly light. 'I am thankful we have rescued her before a major storm occurs. It has been an expensive and time-consuming operation for the British military forces, but I have been told there will be no salvage claim against me. This is a kind and generous gesture and I am very grateful for all they have done.'

After spending three more days in the shelter of Stanley harbour alongside the tug *Salvageman*, whose crew repaired his self-steering, generator and forestays, the New Zealander set sail again on 4 April, reaching Rio on 22 April, twelve days after the fleet had left on the last leg back to Newport.

Opposite, bottom: Richard Konkolski, the third across the line on the last leg, being greeted by his wife at the finish.

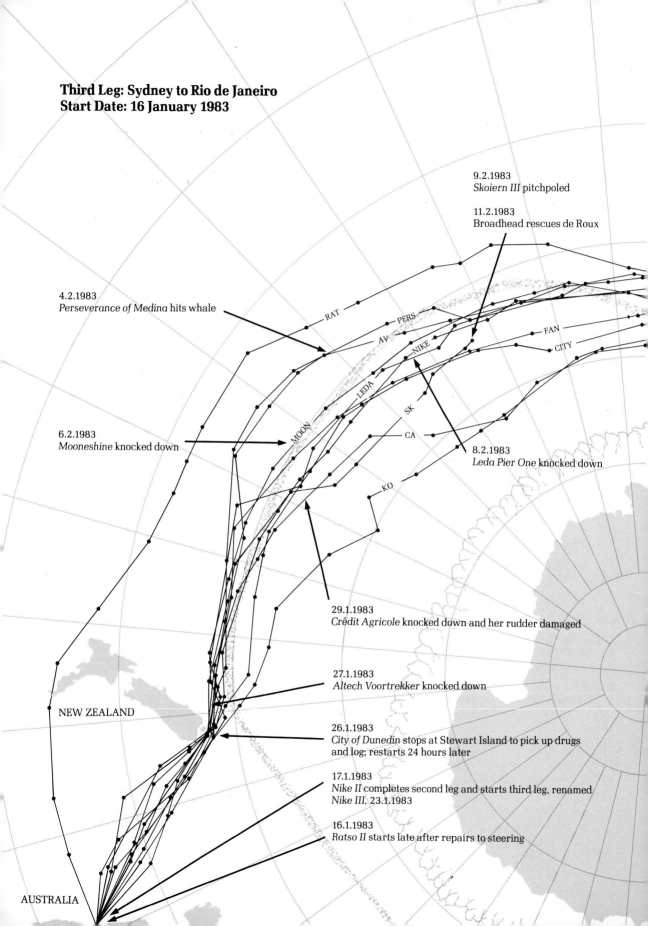

Third Leg: Sydney to Rio de Janeiro
Start Date: 16 January 1983

9.2.1983
Skoiern III pitchpoled

11.2.1983
Broadhead rescues de Roux

4.2.1983
Perseverance of Medina hits whale

RAT

PERS

AV

NIKE

FAN

CITY

LEDA

MOON

SK

6.2.1983
Mooneshine knocked down

CA

8.2.1983
Leda Pier One knocked down

KO

29.1.1983
Crédit Agricole knocked down and her rudder damaged

27.1.1983
Altech Voortrekker knocked down

NEW ZEALAND

26.1.1983
City of Dunedin stops at Stewart Island to pick up drugs
and log; restarts 24 hours later

17.1.1983
Nike II completes second leg and starts third leg, renamed
Nike III, 23.1.1983

16.1.1983
Ratso II starts late after repairs to steering

AUSTRALIA

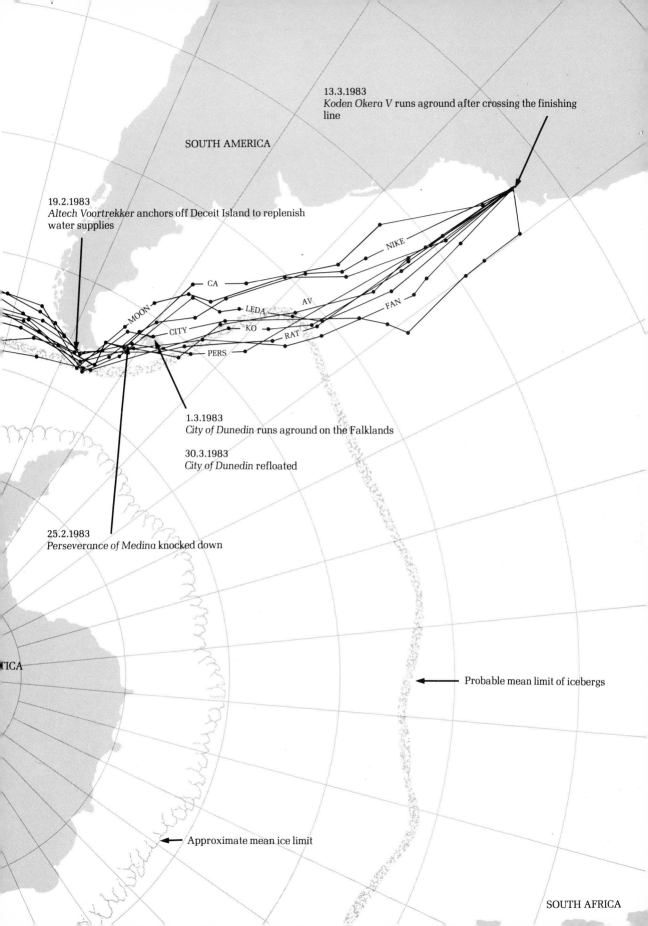

SOUTH AMERICA

13.3.1983
Koden Okera V runs aground after crossing the finishing line

19.2.1983
Altech Voortrekker anchors off Deceit Island to replenish water supplies

NIKE

CA

AV

MOON

LEDA

FAN

CITY

KO

RAT

PERS

1.3.1983
City of Dunedin runs aground on the Falklands

30.3.1983
City of Dunedin refloated

25.2.1983
Perseverance of Medina knocked down

ICA

Probable mean limit of icebergs

Approximate mean ice limit

SOUTH AFRICA

Fourth Leg:
Rio de Janeiro to Newport

'Mañana' may not be a part of the local vocabulary, but its meaning is certainly well established in Rio's rich pattern of life. In any other port, this 'Brazilian Factor', as it became known among the nine BOC survivors, would have driven them to despair. But here in the tranquil surroundings of the world's most expensive yacht club, where staff almost outnumber the members, the frustrations of continual delays and broken pledges with the promise that things would always be right tomorrow were somehow dissolved by the sweet smiles of the hosts and thoughts of another round of refreshments.

The decision to hold a lengthy sojourn in the sun so close to the delights of Copacabana Beach – amounting to five weeks for the leaders – had been taken originally to give the tail-enders time to recuperate after their extended rigours in the Southern Ocean and to

The Rio Yacht Club, one of the most exclusive in the world and boasting every facility, which was host to the fleet in Brazil.

prepare their yachts for the final 5300-mile leg back to Newport. It was just as well, too, for this lazy, carefree life was as infectious as the bouts of 'Rio's Revenge' that attacked all at some point during their stay. By the end, when the travelhoist used to lift the yachts in and out of the water had broken down for the umpteenth time and the lack of spare parts looked like leaving half the fleet high and dry for the scheduled start on 10 April, the skippers had become so conditioned that most merely shrugged their shoulders, content to let time decide. At any other port, Dan Byrne would have shown more concern when he found, after *Fantasy* had been lifted, that her rudder had all but seized up. A repair was promised, but whether it was done in time was a matter he knew was in the lap of the gods. 'Ah, well', he told me with a resigned sigh three days before the start, 'Who needs a rudder anyway? I could do this last leg in a dinghy.'

Bertie Reed, who was lying second in Class 1, at the start of the last leg.

Bertie Reed, now trailing Philippe Jeantot by more than ten days on elapsed time and virtually resigned to finish second, was less complacent. He had used his time ashore to refurbish *Voortrekker's* gear and paintwork, but expressed concern before the restart for her rigging, especially the backstay which was now showing signs of stretch. 'I'm going to be taking it very easily over this last stage of the race', he said, knowing full well that a simple breakage could yet decide first – or even second – place.

Four days before the fleet left Rio, the Committee deducted 145 hours from Richard Broadhead's elapsed time to compensate him for the time he lost rescuing Jacques de Roux during the third leg. Their decision took account not only of the time the Englishman lost when turning back but of the adverse change in conditions he met after de Roux had been transferred to the frigate *Henry*. The allowance had the effect of placing Broadhead the distance he might reasonably have been expected to be behind Bertie Reed when the South African rounded Cape Horn had the rescue not taken place, and this strengthened the Englishman's hold on third place overall, ahead of Neville Gosson, who also received a 21-hour allowance for the part he played during the rescue.

Francis Stokes cleaning oil off *Mooneshine*. At the start of the fourth leg he trailed Yukoh Tada by 50 hours for the Class 2 overall honours.

If the pecking order among the Class 1 yachts now seemed beyond doubt, the leading protagonists in Class 2 still had everything to play for. All that divided Yukoh Tada's 13.41-m (44-ft) *Koden Okera V* from the smaller *Mooneshine* of Francis Stokes was fifty hours, promising a close contest on the last stage of the voyage for the $25,000 prize money. Knowing that headwinds were expected at least as far as the Equator, the Japanese sailor employed his time ashore filling *Okera's* sheet steel keel above the lead bulb with polyurethene foam in the hope that the rough aerofoil section he finished up with would somehow improve the yacht's windward performance. Though pleased with his handiwork after the foam had been sheathed in glassfibre, the finished section was far from uniform and was to contribute to a marked reduction in the yacht's performance.

At Rio Richard Konkolski spent a frantic week stripping down *Nike III*'s engine to replace the bearings ruined as a result of a knock down on the second leg.

Nike III was another hive of activity during this stopover, for Richard Konkolski, encouraged by his performance on the third leg after the poor showing on the first half of the circumnavigation, was determined now to finish the race on a high note. More than a tonne of surplus equipment was discarded on the quayside in a drastic effort to lessen the yacht's displacement for this light weather leg home, and he also removed the steel fins fitted to her transom in Cape Town, which had been designed to improve directional stability in the Southern Ocean. He would have discarded the engine too if it had not started the night before the race was due to resume. Much to everyone's surprise, including the Czech's, it fired on the button after he had spent a frantic week re-building it after replacing bearings ruined as a result of that knockdown during the second leg.

Start day came all too soon for most competitors. All wanted to finish the Challenge, but the departure from the carnival atmosphere generated in this sun-drenched South American resort was a wrench. Neville Gosson was one who would happily have stayed for a lifetime, and he might have been given the opportunity had Yukoh Tada's *Koden Okera V* rammed *Leda Pier One* harder than she did, moments before the five-minute gun. It took some time for the two to disentangle themselves, and though the Australian yacht was one of the first to cross the line at the leeward end, the fact that her skipper had still to set his light genoa quickly dropped her out of the reckoning.

Sail up or not, the Australian would probably have dropped back anyway, for starting where he did, *Leda*, and most of the other yachts for that matter, were outside an invisible slant in the wind which gave *Nike III* an immediate advantage at the opposite end of the line, lifting her a good 10° higher into the fresher breeze outside the bay. Lucky break or not, Konkolski capitalised on this good fortune to the full, for the commanding lead he built up was not challenged until *Nike* was well on her way towards Cabo Frio, where the longer legs of *Crédit Agricole* and *Altech Voortrekker* gave them the advantage over the smaller Class 2 boat.

With more than 1000 miles of windward work ahead of them before any could expect to ease sheets around Brazil's bulging coastline, most skippers, fearful of following Hampton and McBride on to the rocks – or worse, being run down by an unobservant ship in this busy sea lane – now slept in their cockpits rather than below in order to keep a better watch. For Dan Byrne, the lesson to keep a constant watch, if lesson were needed, was given to him three days out. He wrote in his diary:

> I was on the radio talking to Francis Stokes on *Mooneshine* when I felt *Fantasy* begin to hobby-horse as if she were crossing choppy water. I was mildly curious. Without alarm, and unhurriedly, I went topside to have a look. I was stunned to see the long, low outline of the tanker *Northern Lion* dead ahead and hardly more than a stone's throw away. The hobby-horsing I

Nike III, still showing the scars from her time ashore, led the fleet across the starting line on the final leg back to Newport.

felt was the tanker's bow wave fanning out as it passed. We were that close – about 180 m (200 yards). It was daylight. They certainly saw me and almost certainly altered course to miss me. But what if it had been night and they had not seen me? Seventy-five thousand tons of tanker would not transmit the slightest sound to those on the bridge when it hit and sank me.

Throughout that first week, the fleet was bedevilled by 0–10 knot winds, mainly from the north-east, as they short-tacked their way close in towards the coastline to avoid the Brazilian Current. Not surprisingly perhaps, Philippe Jeantot led the fray once more, but less expected was the fine performance maintained by Richard Konkolski whose 13.41-m (44-ft) *Nike* trailed the Frenchman by just 12 miles at this stage of the leg. The two had managed to complete little more than 800 miles that week, only half the average *Crédit Agricole* had set over the rest of the voyage, but it was still twice the distance covered by the back markers *Fantasy* and *Koden Okera*. Trailing the Czech by an unaccustomed 40 miles was Bertie Reed, but such had been the light air lottery during those first few days that the South African had himself shared the lead, then lost it again with a change in the wind.

Once past Recife, conditions and current changed for the better and by the following weekend, Philippe Jeantot was within 2500 miles of the Newport finish line, having slipped through the Doldrums without a halt to lead Reed by a 200-mile margin, with Richard Broadhead a further 160 miles astern. The 15–20 knot reaching winds these three enjoyed helped them to stretch ahead of Konkolski, who figured in his own 24-hour drama at the end of that second week. At 17.25 GMT on Friday, 22 April, the signal from *Nike's* Argos transmitter went dead, and this, plus his silence on the daily inter-yacht radio chat, forced race headquarters in Newport to raise the alarm. If it had been any other competitor the Committee might have held their hand but ever since the start, when it became common knowledge that the Czech intended to seek asylum on his return to America, the fear that one of the Eastern bloc navies might attempt to intercept his yacht during the race had led the committee to fudge *Nike's* true position when publicising the fleet standings each week and made them worry for his safety now.

Had *Nike* been subjected to a little Red target practice, or run down in the busy shipping lanes north of Brazil? The Committee had no way of knowing and no alternative but to order a search. Neville Gosson's *Leda Pier One*, 60 miles to the north-east of *Nike's* last known position, proved to be the nearest yacht and was diverted to join in the search with the Brazilian Navy and coastguard services, despite reservations on the seriousness of the situation felt by others in the race. Richard Broadhead was one who had reservations; he wrote in his log that day:

> *Nike III* did not come up on schedule and his Argos has ceased transmitting. Neville has turned back to his last position, which is about 50 miles off coast. Race Committee are acting too fast. His radio was on the blink yesterday and maybe the Argos has gone on the blink also. Additionally, why send Nev back who has limited horizon? Aircraft could do the job far easier and better, for there is no Mayday position to send Nev to – only a broad area. Case of over-reacting – no search should be invoked without a Mayday or other concrete evidence of distress.

These doubts were to prove correct, for twenty-four hours later, Konkolski came up as normal on the radio net wondering what all the fuss was about. He had not come up on the air waves the previous day, because he had been stripping his set down to investigate the earlier malfunction, and as for the loss of signals from his Argos, he suggested that a sail laid over the transponder might somehow have shielded its transmission from the satellites above. Gosson was able to resume racing, but having now dropped to fifth position, a good 430 miles behind *Crédit Agricole*, his abortive mission had an unfortunate effect on the close contest he had been having with Richard Broadhead.

Whether this possibility of international intrigue played on Dan Byrne's subconscious that weekend is unknown, but the strange emergence of a fishing boat shadowing *Fantasy's* course 15 days from Rio had him troubled, as can be seen from his diary:

> For the first time in the voyage, I was frightened last night. A strange boat followed me for an hour, gradually overtaking me. It was a diesel and by its lights, a fisherman, about 15 m (50 ft) long. I tried to raise him on the VHF, but got no reply. Still he came closer. Piracy remains a fact of life on the oceans of the world. So I was not being skittish in my concern and growing alarm as the strange vessel came steadily closer, doing 8 knots to

Dan Byrne resorted to transmitting a radio message to an imaginary companion yacht when he feared that he was being pursued by a pirate vessel close to the equator. Perhaps the possibility of there being another yacht in the vicinity discouraged the occupants of the vessel from taking aggressive action.

my 6. I kept turning up towards the wind and the east. He turned with me. I could not turn any further lest I head directly into the wind and stop dead. I prepared to close and lock the hatch and seal myself on board.

I went on the VHF again. This time I had a one-sided conversation with an imaginery yacht that I pretended I was sailing with and that, I said on the air, was 10 miles away. I hoped that onboard the mystery vessel, they would blame their antenna for not picking up my 'companion' boat. 'Bill and John are sleeping below', I said. Then I matter of factly mentioned the boat that was gaining on me, describing its lights and speed. I had no way of knowing if this bit of radio drama had the slightest effect on my pursuer. I do know that he finally came about 45 m (50 yards) abeam of me on my port side, passed me, turned across my bow and headed due east. I watched his floodlit stern deck recede into the night for an hour. That was the final mystery.

Another mystery that third week surrounded Yukoh Tada's poor performance on this leg. The Japanese sailor had barely been able to keep up even with *Fantasy* during the first two weeks and, now trailing 160 miles astern of Francis Stokes, looked to have lost his grip on the $25,000 prize. He complained that since making those modifications to her keel, *Koden Okera* had proved unmanageable in headwinds but he hoped his fortunes might improve now that she was enjoying fresh south-easterly reaching winds and moving well at 8 knots or more.

Neville Gosson's *Leda Pier One* was called to divert to the last known position of *Nike III* when Richard Konkolski failed to come up on the radio and his Argos stopped transmitting on the same day. Gosson spent 24 hours searching during the false alarm.

The following Thursday, 28 April, Richard McBride set out from Rio, nineteen days behind the fleet, suffering from the statutory bout of 'Rio's Revenge' but otherwise keen to complete the course. One of the last-minute details had been to have his ear pierced – the only competitor to do so – and he set out proudly wearing the sailor's gold ear-ring that traditionally marks a 'Cape Horner' and which was presented by BOC to all the competitors when they reached Brazil. With more than 2000 miles separating *City of Dunedin* from the tail-enders in the fleet there was no chance for him to finish higher than tenth overall, but the New Zealander was philosophical about it all. He wrote in his log during his second day at sea:

> It's pleasant to contemplate log and sailing intructions – 'Fourth leg'! So nearly wasn't possible. I'm not tired of it yet, but all the same will be glad to reach Newport and relax the pressure a bit. Although I am not in contention for a prize, I'm still sailing as hard as possible because it's the only logical way to sail ... bashing to windward of course is better over and done with as soon as possible.

Richard McBride, who set out from Rio 19 days behind the fleet, contemplating the final leg at the cluttered chart table of *City of Dunedin*.

At the end of that third week Jeantot had extended his lead to a 400-mile margin, and the widening gap stung Bertie Reed to greater efforts. When the wind freed sufficiently to set a spinnaker during his twenty-fifth day at sea and he found that the Atom self-steering could not handle the extra strain, he took over the helm himself, staying at the tiller for 20 hours in an effort to squeeze an extra knot out of the 16-year-old boat. He did well, too, for with Jeantot running short of wind as *Crédit Agricole* approached the American seaboard, the South African narrowed the lead at one point to within 90 miles, but by then the Frenchman was almost home.

Jeantot had hoped to combine victory celebrations with his 31st birthday but light winds eventually delayed his arrival off the Brenton Tower finish line until the following day, Monday, 9 May. But crossing the line shortly after dawn at 07.11 local time he still broke the record for the circumnavigation held previously by the late Alain Colas by a massive nine-day margin. In fact a further four hours could have been pared from his record time of 159 days 2 hours 26 minutes, but having missed his birthday deadline by two hours, and arriving at each of the other ports of call at night, he decided, much to the annoyance of the army of French journalists and photographers who had flown across specially to record the momentous occasion, to lie hove-to a few miles from the finish and wait for daylight before crossing the line. Emerging from a bank of fog looking fit and relaxed – which was more than could be said for the 200 pressmen who had waited all night in the heaving swell – the Frenchman finally won the race he had dominated throughout in the grandest style, to a welter of shouts and applause from the hundreds who lined the dockside to greet him.

He was joined almost exactly twenty-four hours later by the man who had chased him into every port but now trailed by more than 11

Left: Philippe Jeantot celebrates his record-breaking circumnavigation of the world, in which he beat by a massive 10-day margin the previous best time, set in 1973–74 by fellow Frenchman Alain Colas on *Manureva*, a trimaran nearly 4.8 m (14 ft) longer than *Crédit Agricole*.

Below: Jeantot missed by a matter of two hours combining victory in The BOC Challenge with the celebration of his thirty-first birthday and decided to delay crossing the finishing line until the morning of 9 May 1983, making this the first time he had completed a leg in daylight.

**Left: Bertie Reed
providing a helping hand
to take down
Perseverance of Medina's
sails after Richard
Broadhead crossed the
finishing line to take third
place overall.**

**Right: Neville Gosson,
who had been enjoying a
close tussle with Richard
Broadhead for third place
before being called to
search for *Nike III*, was
awarded a time
allowance that gave him a
time equal to Broadhead
on this stage of the race.**

days on elapsed time. For Reed it had been the easiest of the four legs, but he did have a couple of scary moments. 'Two nights ago a whale tried to make love to me', he told us at an impromptu press conference held on the dockside. 'I could see it in the phosphorescence swimming underneath the yacht and had to start the engine to scare it away.' He had also been worried when he saw a ship heading straight towards him the same night, for having shorted out his batteries he had no reserve power for *Voortrekker*'s navigation lights or the radio to warn the ship's bridge of his position, but thankfully a collision was avoided.

Finishing with an elapsed time of 170 days 16 hours 51 minutes, the South African was handicapped from the outset by the size of his elderly yacht, the smallest in Class 1, which at 14.93 m (49 ft) was just not big enough to compete on equal terms with Jeantot's maxi. However, when one takes into account that he did not have an effective self-steering system for running or reaching in heavy weather, all credit should go to this tough Simonstown sailing instructor for staying ahead of his six other rivals in this class throughout the eight-month circumnavigation. Statistics can bolster any argument, but it is interesting when comparing the performances of the first and second finishers to note that Philippe Jeantot's average speed was only 2.73 miles per day faster than the South African's, who, had he chosen to follow the Frenchman's significantly shorter course – 26,500 miles against an estimated distance of 27,100 miles – might have narrowed the overall time difference to 2 days 16 hours.

The two were joined on Goat Island at 1.13 am on Friday, 13 May by the 'unluckiest' competitor in the race, Richard Konkolski. In Rio, he had said that fate had been totally against him on the first half of the voyage, but from Sydney onwards his record time of 84 days, 16 hours was 9 hours faster than any of his nearest Class 2 rivals, and enough to pull him up from last to third overall. His luck held right to the end, too, for having stayed neck and neck with Richard Broadhead for most of the last leg from Rio, he won the light air lottery at the end, finishing hours ahead of the Englishman, who, caught up in the Gulf Stream without wind, was pushed too far to the north.

Perseverance of Medina finally crossed the line early on the afternoon of Sunday 15 May and her skipper was treated to a standing ovation from 200 well-wishers in recognition of the skill and seamanship he had displayed when rescuing Jacques de Roux during the third leg. His elapsed time of 192 days 10 hours and 6 minutes might have been 33 days outside the time set by Jeantot, but it was enough to give him third overall by a ten-day margin over the Australian Neville Gosson, who finished a day later. Until the false alarm over Konkolski's well-being, the two had been enjoying a close tussle for third place in their class on this leg, and sensing perhaps the injustice to both sailors if the time allowance given to Gosson after his diversion changed the result, the Committee finally decided to make the two third equal.

Shortly after 8.30 pm that same day, Monday, 16 May, Francis Stokes chased the Australian across the line to become the sixth to finish but his time of 209 days 1 hours 32 minutes for the circumnavigation was 35 hours short of beating Yukoh Tada whose arrival the next morning assured him of Class 2 honours.

'Francis is better sailor', Tada said about his American friend. 'This is the biggest fluke in my life. I did not mean to win. It is the first time in my life I am a winner.' But Robin Knox-Johnston was there to put the record straight about the shy saxophone-playing taxi driver, whose love for modern art, jazz and saki made him one of the principal characters of the race. 'No; Yukoh, the best man won and you deserve all the credit,' which drew a giggle and shy bow from the man who probably made most friends during the race.

A day later Guy Bernardin made it eight home, finishing in the dead of night to a loud welcome from his wife and friends. 'I did it for Jacques,' The Frenchman told me after docking *Ratso* alongside the jetty at Goat Island. 'For this last leg I renamed the boat in my

Guy Bernardin arriving
at Newport after an
exhilerating final stretch.

mind 'Spirit of Skoiern' and sailed her as fast as I could.' Finishing
fourth overall in Class 2, he said of the result: 'I am disappointed, but
also pleased with myself. I did the maximum I could with the
smallest boat.'

Dan Byrne had hoped to finish shortly after the Frenchman but a
frustrating battle against a dying wind, just as he had had at Cape
Town, Sydney and Rio, set him back once more. 'The last few weeks
have been miserable,' he said after finally reaching the Brenton Reef
Light at 6.17 am on 20 May. 'These finishes are just driving me
crazy.' But it hadn't just been the breeze that had affected *Fantasy*'s
progress, for the day before arriving off Newport she had tangled
with another problem. Byrne noted in his diary:

What an ordeal! Only thirty-seven miles from noon to noon. The
sea was like glass last night. I woke this morning to notice the
knotmeter was reading zero and yet the sails were full and
pulling in a slight breeze. Then I saw that my rudder had
snagged a lobster pot line. I saw a fisherman cruising about two
miles off and tried calling him on the VHF, but got no response.

I dropped all sail and tried to free the line, without success.
Finally, feeling guilty, I got my scuba knife and cut the line.

About an hour later, I was blasted out of my seat at the chart
table by several short bursts of a horn very close by. I dashed
topside expecting to see a ship about to run me down. Instead,
close alongside was the fishing boat. The crew waved a lobster
and asked me if I wanted one. I declined. I wonder if that was
the owner of the trap I cut?

The 56-year-old former newspaper editor was nevertheless
ecstatic after completing the Challenge – something he had held
private doubts about before the start – and catching a glimpse of

A jubilant Dan Byrne, finishing in ninth place overall. At early stages in the race he thought he would not be able to measure up to the challenge.

Prize-giving at the end of the final leg. Left to right: Yukoh Tada, Bertie Reed, Dan Byrne, Francis Stokes, Richard Konkolski, Philippe Jeantot, Guy Bernardin, Richard Broadhead and Neville Gosson.

David White standing on the dockside to welcome him, he called over: 'Hey David, it's one hell of an idea you had.'

It was a view endorsed by all the competitors, not least Richard McBride, who eventually made it across the finish line on 6 June, nine months and nine days after the start. For this New Zealander more than any other perhaps, the race had proved an uphill struggle from the outset, but while others fell by the wayside, his dogged determination to overcome all odds and adversities to finish the race served as a lesson in life that all were to admire – and that, of course, was what the BOC Challenge was really all about.

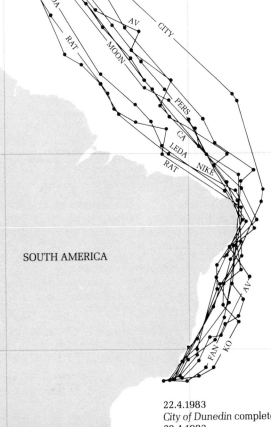

NORTH AMERICA

**Fourth Leg: Rio de Janeiro to Newport
Start Date: 10 April 1983**

SOUTH AMERICA

22.4.1983
City of Dunedin completes third leg and starts fourth leg
28.4.1983

Left: Yukoh Tada cutting off the special bowsprit fitted to *Koden Okera V* to ward off icebergs in the Southern Ocean.

Below: The solar panels fitted around the cockpit of Dan Byrne's *Fantasy*.

Lessons in Gear and Equipment

If radios and the regular link they gave competitors with each other and the outside world alleviated the distressing effects of loneliness, all thanks are due to the world-wide net of amateur 'ham' radio operators who kept a continuous link with the BOC fleet throughout the 27,000-mile marathon.

During previous endurance races, competitors had always used commercial channels, which proved to be both expensive, time-consuming and inefficient. Anyone who has ventured well offshore and had to make a call over their SSB radio will know the frustrations involved. The delay in being linked through a commercial station can take two hours or more, and limited fuel stocks have to be burnt to keep batteries charged while what appears to be the entire passenger list on the QE2 and countless merchantmen hold conversations with their loved ones. And even when the calls are eventually patched through, poor reception often makes them unintelligible, especially when deep in the Southern Ocean, as radio operators on competing yachts in past Whitbread round-the-world races found, despite the use of powerful transmitters in excess of 400 watts PEP.

It was for this reason that the BOC Race Committee gave competitors a largely free hand to decide their own transmission frequencies. Most chose 'ham' sets with a powerful output of between 100–150 watts PEP, costing one-tenth of some commercial radios used in previous round-the-world races. To their delight all the BOC competitors found that the 'amateur net' cut out the time delays, proved more reliable and provided a better performance than the commercial alternatives.

Left: The well-equipped navigation area of Yukoh Tada's *Kodera Okera V.*

Opposite: The sheets and control lines on *Crédit Agricole* were colour-coded and ran back to the cockpit so that Jeantot did not have to go on deck to reef or change sails.

Why should there be such a difference?

'The problem lies with the regulations governing commercial transceivers,' was the answer from one leading retailer. 'In order to get an approved certificate, commercial equipment has to be idiot-proof so that the licensed operators, who often have little more than minimal qualifications, have just to dial the correct frequency before transmitting,' he explained. 'The ham network, on the other hand, which links more than a million highly qualified amateur enthusiasts world wide, many of whom assemble their own equipment, provides a keenness and sense of purpose that is not always found on the commercial airwaves. Being enthusiasts they are continually tweeking and tuning their sets during transmission to obtain the maximum efficiency from them. By choosing the right frequencies to suit the time of day, weather and distance involved, a ham can often obtain as good reception with a 50- to 100-watt transmitter as radio operators did working through the commercial frequencies during the 1981/2 Whitbread race with their 800-watt radios costing ten times as much', he said.

'Choosing the right frequency is much more important than transmitting power', another expert explained. 'A ham can often get through to a counterpart on the opposite side of the world with a 50-watt set better than a sailor with a much more powerful radio who is limited to broadcasting on a fixed but poor commercial frequency. In fact, using a powerful radio like that is sometimes akin to hitting a nut with a sledge hammer, and then only giving it a glancing blow.'

This world-wide club has been responsible for saving many lives but it was only in this BOC race that the ham network had been used successfully as a semi-official communications network afloat. The lynch-pin in all these communications was Rob Koziomkowski, a Vietnam war veteran, who with a band of fellow hams in France, South Africa, Australia, New Zealand and South America, managed to maintain a regular link between Race Control and the fleet. Without them, two lives might have been lost during the race and third competitor, Bertie Reed, would probably have been forced to pull out with a gangrenous arm during the second leg. Indeed, so impressed was the South African by the tireless dedicaton displayed by these amateurs that he suggested later that any yachts drawing any distance offshore should always operate on ham frequencies.

Another lesson learnt during the race was the general fallibility of self-steering equipment, both mechanical and electrical. With the exception of the Australian-made Flemming wind vane self-steering gear fitted on *Leda Pier One*, *Koden Okera V* and *Perseverance of Medina* and the Gunning rig on *Gipsy Moth V*, the other similar systems proved just not strong enough to cope in heavy conditions. Significantly perhaps, Dan Byrne and Francis Stokes, sailing long-keeled cruising yachts of similar design which proved to have better directional stability than some of the IOR-influenced designs, succeeded in rounding the globe with relatively little trouble from

The Aries wind-vane self-steering system on *Crédit Agricole* was linked directly to the deck-sweeping tiller. Her electronic self-steering aids were connected by rubber belts to the wheel, which was mounted on a pedestal in the cockpit.

their British-made Aries equipment, the most popular gear before the start. So did race winner Philippe Jeantot, although all three relied equally on electronic self-steering aids. The Frenchman only used his wind vane self-steering when conditions were ideal – moderate to strong headwinds. He relied on an Autohelm 3000 electronic autopilot and a large supply of spare rubber belts to steer a chosen compass course upwind in light weather, or whenever the wind was aft of the beam. *Voortrekker* was equipped with Plastimo electronic steering aid designed for connection to a tiller but this did not prove strong enough for the 14.93 m (49 ft) yacht and eventually broke down during the third leg, as did the larger Autohelm unit on *Crédit Agricole*.

Left: Solar panels provided an effective means of generating electricty on a number of the yachts. These four Motorolo panels mounted on the coach roof of *Crédit Agricole* produced 10 amps per hour on sunny days.

Right: The Proengin roller reefing gear fitted to the headstay and inner forestay of *Crédit Agricole* worked well throughout the circumnavigation.

One of the problems with electronic devices such as these is that their high consumption places a heavy drain on batteries, making the solo sailor heavily reliant on his yacht's charging facilities, which proved less than reliable in some cases. *Crédit Agricole's* auxiliary was backed up by four large Motorolo solar panels mounted on the coachroof, which worked well throughout the voyage, producing 10amps/hour whenever the sun shone. On cloudy days the Frenchman relied on a water-driven Wattas generator which produced 15amps/hour when the yacht was sailing at seven knots or more. In most cases the solar panel technology worked well, although parts of the bracketry holding the panels on Dan Byrne's *Fantasy* did fold during the race. One of these panels, which were prototypes given to him for testing, did show signs of water seepage at Sydney (possibly because of the way the panels were positioned) and was replaced. Another, mounted flush on *Voortrekker's* deck between her two cockpits, stopped functioning, but Reed felt this might have been due to the fact that it had not been fitted with a fuse or cut-out.

The race leaders made extensive use of their spinnakers during the 27,000-mile race and did not shy from carrying them at night, even in the Southern Ocean when conditions permitted. Most skippers employed spinnaker socks to control these sails when hoisting and retrieving them, the exception being Neville Gosson, who set his chutes stopped in rubber bands and hauled them back in hand-over-hand because he had been unable to find a successful sock design before the race in his native Australia. *Crédit Agricole*, whose sails were all supplied by Hood, also carried two heavy weather 'booster sails' – boomed out running sails – whose luffs were set in the twin-grooved Proengin headsail foil which, the Frenchman reported, helped to steady the yacht when conditions in the South Ocean became too much for a spinnaker.

Lack of finance was the root cause of many problems experienced during the race. This was particularly so in the case of Neville Gosson's *Leda Pier One*, which suffered continual fatigue problems with her rig. She is shown here with her forestay lying broken on the deck after arriving in Cape Town with failed roller reefing gear and a broken strand to her starboard cap shroud.

Headsail furling gear proved to be essential. Every time Bertie Reed was forced to fight his way forward to change down to a smaller headsail during heavy weather, he thought of his French rival ahead, sitting in the safety of *Crédit Agricole's* cockpit merely pulling on a control line to effect a similar change in sail area. The hefty Proengin roller reefing gear fitted to both the headstay and inner forestay on the French yacht worked well throughout the voyage but some other skippers experienced continual troubles with other makes of this type of equipment. One in particular was Neville Gosson, though to be totally objective, the Australian did not have the latest designs and was troubled throughout the voyage by fatigued rigging which would have been replaced before the start had he had the finance available. Lack of finance was the root cause of so many problems experienced by others during the race.

At a press conference held immediately after his arrival, Jeantot credited part of his success to the Danavigate 7000 computerised instrumentation system which, linked to a fire bell, could be set to wake him whenever course, boatspeed, windspeed or direction moved outside the margins set in the computer's memory, and in a reference to *Gipsy Moth's* sad demise on Gabo Island, the Frenchman said that if Hampton had had this or similar equipment installed, he would probably have finished the race!

Lessons in Human Responses

If prisoners of war faced the same mental and physical torture that the seventeen BOC sailors had to stand up to – the effects of solitary confinement, intense discomfort and disturbed sleep, not to mention experiences where life itself is threatened – the world those competitors were trying to circumnavigate would be outraged. Yet the race brought hardly a murmur on the subject; just an air of incredulity that people might choose to face such pressures voluntarily and the suggestion that all were perhaps a little mad to attempt the Challenge in the first place.

But none of them was mad. They merely sought a challenge that would test them to their limits – and beyond. Each wanted to experience the personal satisfaction of facing up to themselves. They might have chosen to climb Everest or walk to the North Pole. Instead they undertook the world's loneliest and most arduous voyage knowing that they risked no one but themselves. It takes tremendous strength and willpower first to decide on such an undertaking, then to see it through to the bitter end. It is perhaps a deep-rooted question mark over our own 'normal' staying power that leads us to consider mad those who attempt to succeed at something most of us would never think of doing ourselves.

This view is strengthened by the findings of Dr Lawrence W. Kneisley MD from the Torrence Sleep Disorders Centre, California and Marsha E. Grant RN, who made a study of the competitors' changing moods and sleep patterns during The BOC Challenge. Before the start, they examined eleven of the sixteen contestants, subjecting each to a psychological test, then interviewed them again in Cape Town and Rio before and after their experiences in the Southern Ocean. Their fascinating paper reveals the strong psychological pressures these sailors faced and came through without cracking up.[1] They wrote:

> In contrast to the guarded but confident rhetoric of the weeks in Newport we saw men whose emotions while alone ranged from impulsive, child-like anger, even rage, to fear, apathy and depression. Some sailors' apathy became so severe that routine chores were not done, dirty boats were left uncleaned for weeks, and long gaps would appear in logs or personal journals. Dan Byrne's personal journal of the second leg, published in *U.S.A. Today*,[2] was most revealing. After returning to Capetown for repairs he restarted and after a brief euphoric afternoon sank into what I believe is a state of apathetic depression. After a ten-day hiatus in his journal, he wrote (day 21): 'This is the first I have written in days. I have been alternately depressed, anxious, frustrated and apathetic, but to keep my spirits up, I have to keep busy. One of the actions I must take is working on this log. A week later (Day 28) he wrote: 'Emotionally this leg is much

worse than Newport to Cape Town. I have been depressed, discouraged, frightened and generally disenchanted. I was sailing sloppily. I would stay in one tack for too long when the other tack was favoured for my course. I would delay taking down sail when the wind came up; and I would procrastinate about putting sail up when the wind decreased.'

Loss of Sleep

Sleep, or rather the lack of it, had the most dramatic effect on the sailors' mental state and behaviour patterns. Before the race, Dr Glin Bennet MD, who has conducted extensive research into the performance of sailors at sea, warned in an article published in The BOC Challenge Programme:[3]

> After one night with only two hours' sleep or after two consecutive nights with five hours each, some impairment of efficiency can be expected. When one whole night has been spent awake, even a full night's sleep is not sufficient to restore the person to full efficiency. Practically speaking, sailors engaged in the absorbing task of steering a boat in a storm for hours on end will be functioning at a lower level of efficiency than they suppose, and they will also be doing everything much more slowly than when rested.

Kneisley and Grant's findings show that while most of the competitors got 75–90 per cent of their normal land-based 'sleep requirement' during the first leg, the story was very different on the second stage of the voyage, when conditions in the notorious Roaring Forties and Screaming Fifties stretched some to their limits of endurance.

> In the second leg several boats lost their self-steering. Richard Konkolski, Bertie Reed and Richard Broadhead had to hand steer 14–18 hours per day under cold and difficult conditions. They greatly reduced their nocturnal sleep time (to 2–4 hours) since their boats were essentially 'hove-to' or moving very slowly under reduced sail while they slept. When *Altech Voortrekker's* self-steering was working, Bertie Reed usually took a two-hour afternoon nap and stayed up late into the night, a habit he developed in the OSTAR and continued on land when possible. None of the other sailors napped regularly during the day. Most said that they got up with the sun and went below with the sun. When near land or in one case near icebergs, all slept mostly at night. Nocturnal sleep was usually interrupted to varying degrees. More competitive, highly disciplined racers woke themselves with an alarm at regular intervals every 20–90 minutes throughout the night. About half the racers woke either spontaneously or by alarm 1–4 times per night. In calm or light conditions far from shipping lanes or land, many made no effort to waken themselves with an alarm and would depend on spontaneous awakenings which occurred irregularly.

All said they could 'feel' changes in boat heel or boat motion and would waken from sleep.

When awakened, virtually all the racers would either go up into the cockpit, or poke their heads out of the cabin to look at sail trim, boat heel and to scan the horizon. All had compasses and some had windpoint indicators and other instruments that could be seen from their bunks. A quick look at these with a flashlight while lying in the bunk was often sufficient. When in or near the shipping lanes or near land, the racers woke themselves more frequently, virtually always went on deck to look at the horizon; often a sailor stayed awake all or nearly all of the night in these circumstances. Whether a sailor actually got out of his bunk at night when none of these conditions prevailed seemed to depend on (1) his competitiveness, (2) severe conditions of strong winds, (3) his general level of fatigue.

During the second leg, Richard Broadhead's boat was so cold and wet below that he could hardly sleep. When near the equator during the first leg, nearly all of the sailors found that sleeping in their hot, stuffy boats was uncomfortable and difficult. For this reason, Tony Lush slept virtually the entire first leg in the cockpit. Some slept in different places during rain or heavy spray. For example, during the first leg, David White would sleep forward where he stored his sails so that his foul weather gear and clothes, wet from many trips topside, would not dampen his bunk.

During periods of excessive fatigue, some BOC competitors found that mind and body appeared to separate. Confirming the findings of Kneisley and Grant, Neville Gosson told me in Rio:

There were time during bad weather when I had to work for 24–48 hours at a stretch to steer or repair the boat and became totally exhausted. I became desperate for sleep, but no sooner had I climbed in my bunk then something broke – that's of course when it always happens – but you are so tired you can think of a million reasons why it can wait for another fifteen minutes or an hour. But your mind won't let you. It nags – 'You've got to fix it ... You've got to get up ... You've got to do it now.' It's just like a mother nagging her young – and there is no way you can sleep.

Depression

Depression was another problem every competitor experienced. Neville Gosson spoke of phases every 2–3 days which did not necessarily coincide with problems or bad weather when he would start to think: 'You're wasting your time, you're too far behind.' He would get out of his bunk depressed and stay that way for the rest of the day. 'You don't see nice things when you are depressed,' he explained. 'Everything becomes a hassle or a problem. It even becomes a struggle to get up. You finish up cursing and swearing, and I would even kick the mast a few times in anger.' Bertie Reed spoke of these moods overtaking him every 6–7 days when he found it hard to generate any motivation for a day or more. 'The only way I seemed to work it out of my system was to do some menial chore like tidying up the cabin', he told me during the Sydney stop-over.

Fear
According to the Kneisley/Grant paper the anger that Gosson displayed may have been a defense mechanism against fear:

> Getting angry is often more acceptable to a person than feeling the fear that his anger covers up. The anger in such a case is a defense. Among the BOC racers, anger was very common. 'I kicked the mast and swore and stomped on the deck like a spoiled child', said one. 'I pounded my fists on the deck', said another. 'I was beside myself with frustration ... at the utter contrariness of the winds', reported another. Anger is also a natural reaction to *real* danger. One gets angry at forces which are trying to kill you or sink your boat or leave you stranded in the middle of the ocean. A usually composed racer said in Capetown: 'I'd find myself swearing. I'd become offensive. I don't swear a lot (on land), but I found as the trip got on and I became tireder, I would (say) "F— this", and "F— that", and I'd kick the mast ... I couldn't stop it – no matter what I did.' After *Gladiator* sustained significant damage in the North Atlantic and had to retire, David White, her skipper, became both depressed and enraged, impulsively throwing overboard everything designated 'official'. Dan Byrne, who said he was only occasionally profane, wrote on Day 33 of the first leg that he 'all but screamed with frustration (at the lack of wind)'. Such anger mobilizes energy, and is thus very useful. Fear, by contrast, paralyzes and is thus dangerous to one's survival.

Running aground as Hampton, McBride and Tada did during the race was the greatest fear expressed by most competitors, though a few, confident in their navigation, considered that running into the unexpected – an iceberg or ship – to be the greater threat. No one expressed concern for falling overboard. All appeared confident in their agility and the safety precautions each took when the weather was bad, which included wearing a safety harness.

Understandably, most had deep reservations about climbing the mast while at sea, for all knew that even on a calm day the masthead gyrates alarmingly as the yacht rolls in the swell, to leave them badly shaken and bruised. The competitors employed different methods to reach the top. Some carried rope or wire ladders they hoisted aloft on a halyard which they then tied at intervals to the mast as they climbed aloft. Francis Stokes tied ratlines between the shrouds when he needed to climb up and repair the spreader that split during the first leg while Jeantot employed 'Ascender' mountaineering rope clamps attached to his harness to help him shin up a halyard.

Before the start, Neville Gosson decided that he would go up the mast only as a last resort but so great were the problems experienced with *Leda*'s rig that he had to climb to the top half a dozen times or more before his return to Newport. 'I was not so much scared, more apprehensive and tense', he told me in Rio. 'The violent motion makes you feel sick and want to go to the toilet. I can see where the phrase "It gives you the shits" comes from, because that is exactly what it does to you.'

Some controlled this fear by disciplining themselves, as Kneisley and Grant point out in their paper:

> An example of unconscious denial of fear and fatigue was *extreme rigidity*, i.e. discipline, Jacques de Roux was an extraordinarily disciplined and competitive sailor who, according to his sleep log, woke himself every 30–45 minutes each night of the first leg. De Roux kept a meticulous ship's log in ink without a single cross-out (all the others used pencil). He admitted to no emotional difficulties. Physically, he was well-groomed, in contrast to some of the other racers. His boat was surprisingly tidy; his instruments were neatly and symmetrically mounted in the cabin. It seems highly likely that this extreme rigidity, conspicuous in normal life, saved his life when his boat was dismasted and holed and he had to stay awake to bail by hand for 2½ days until being rescued.

Hallucinations

A number of short-handed and solo sailors have hallucinated during periods of exhaustion. Cornelis van Rietschoten, the Dutch Whitbread Round the World race winner in 1978 and 1982, has recalled how he went into a trance during a harrowing crossing of the North Sea in a Dragon Class keelboat shortly after the Second World War. Cold, wet, hungry and close to exhaustion after facing two days of storms in such a small boat, he became convinced that his sailing companion, sleeping in the cuddy, had gone ashore to buy methylated spirits and that there before him in place of the compass was a plate of bacon and eggs on a well laid table.

In the BOC Programme, Dr Glin Bennet recounts the story of another sailor crossing the North Sea who had difficulty in making out the harbour lights as he approached the Dutch coast after a 40-hour voyage, until he saw two men in yellow oilskins waving to him, indicating the direction he should go. It was only when he drew very close however, that the sailor suddenly realised there were no men, or a jetty, 'only a breakwater of horribly sharp looking sticks'. Bennet uncovered further instances of hallucinations during a study he made of solo sailors competing in the 1972 OSTAR but fears that the BOC sailors would suffer similar problems appear to have been groundless. The Kneisley/Grant paper explains:

> Glin Bennet's now classic study of psychological problems of racers in the 1972 OSTAR[4] described several examples of visual

and auditory hallucinations. Bennet felt that these were due to sleep deprivation, exposure to cold, seasickness, the monotonous noise of wind and possibly isolation from other human contact. In The BOC Challenge, we could not elicit any definite description from the racers of hallucinatory experiences. In spite of long periods of severe or total sleep loss (24–48 hours), when making landfall each sailor denied significant visual or auditory misperceptions. Why the difference? First, all of the racers were familiar with Bennet's work and may have prepared themselves mentally to discount or reject any 'unusual' sights. Second, they were less isolated than were the 1972 OSTAR racers. For many days throughout the race, most of them were in daily or almost daily radio contact with each other or with land. In fact many of the racers structured their daily routine around the 'ham net' or 'chat show' hours. By the end of the second leg, they had become fast friends concerned with each others' safety. Third, during the first leg at least, they were probably better rested than were the OSTAR racers. They were only rarely in shipping lanes except in the few days after leaving or before arriving in a port. Additionally, catching up on sleep was relatively easy in the first leg since the winds were often light and the weather warm. Fourth, each man learned to pace himself for a very long race. Many would reduce sail at night to avoid being wakened unnecessarily. All the racers learned to value a few extra hours of sleep at night above a few extra miles travelled at night, especially in strong winds or big seas. OSTAR was by contrast a 3–5 week 'dash' where every mile counted.

There is no doubt that the race had a profound effect on all ten finishers. As one sailor put it: 'Once you've experienced your first major knockdown in the Southern Ocean and realized just how close you were to the fine divide between life and death, you tend to view life in a very different perspective. Values change, the luxuries we try to surround ourselves with lose all importance, while the basics in life we all take for granted take on a new reality.'

Paul Rodgers who had already made one non-stop circumnavigation before this race astounded other competitors at the start when he claimed that he would never catch fish during the voyage even if he was on the point of starvation. 'Whatever you take from the sea, the sea will take back', was his explanation, and by the race end, the close bond the sailors developed with the sea produced more converts to his belief.

The BOC Challenge had a marked effect on all the competitors and to those who stayed the course it gave a tremendous sense of achievement that others, caught up in one of life's ruts, are unable to appreciate. It was probably for Dan Byrne however, that the race was to produce the most dramatic character change.

Before the start, Byrne, a thrice-married former editor with the *Los Angeles Times* syndicate, displayed all the stressful signs of a hard life in journalism, but by the end the beard he had grown during the voyage masked a totally different personality. Not only had he mellowed considerably, he appeared to have come to terms with himself and life which for him now took on a much wider horizon.

References quoted in the text:
1 Kneisley, Lawrence W. and Grant, Marsha E., Sleep Patterns and Psychological Aspects of The BOC Challenge, to be published.
2 Byrne, D., Diary of a Lone Sailor; Chapter 11, *U.S.A. Today* Section C. Sports, pp. 1C–2C, February 16, 1983.
3 Bennet G., The Challenge of the Mind; Around the World Alone – Official Program – Insert to *Cruising World*, August 1982.
4 Bennet G., Medical and Psychological Problems in the 1972 Single-Handed Transatlantic Yacht Race, *Lancet*, pp. 747–754, 6 October, 1973.

Acknowledgments

The author would particularly like to thank Chris Cunningham, the official photographer, for his considerable help at the start and finish of the race.

Ace Marine Photography: 57 bottom left, 92 top, 120 left; Guy Bernardin: 112, 125 bottom, 131 bottom; Dan Byrne: 115, 126, 134, 146, 159 top; D.H. Clarke: 14, 16; Chris Cunningham: 20, 27 right, 37–9, 42–3, 45 bottom right, 47, 49, 50 bottom, 53, 55, 56 right, 57 top, 57 bottom right, 58, 94, back cover; Guy Ribadeau Dumas: 32; Bruce Hogan: 101–2; Philippe Jeantot: front cover, 60 right, 61, 82, 85, 91, 113, 129, 138–9, 160, 163; Roger Kennedy: 120 right, 141–2, 154, 156, 157 top; Robin Knox-Johnston: 23; James Latter: 92 bottom, 109–10; Tony Lush: 86 top; Richard McBride: 31, 50 top left, 60 left, 77, 86 centre, 87, 90 top, 127, 132, 135, 152, 159 bottom; Bill Mitchell: 28, 56 left; The Observer: 17; Peabody Museum of Salem: 11; Barry Pickthall: 20, 33–5, 46, 50 top right, 51–2, 59, 63, 65, 100 right, 117, 119, 124, 131 top, 147 bottom, 148–9, 151, 164–5; Popperfoto: 18; Bertie Reed: 111, 122, 125 top, 130 bottom; Patrick Riviere: 84, 98, 100 left, 104–5; Paul Rodgers: 2; Stanley Rosenfeld: 45 bottom left, 48–9; John Rubython: 1, 41, 69–71, 74–5, 88–9; Tom Sawyer/ Cruising World Magazine: 27 left; Frieda Squires: 78, 83, 150, 153, 157 bottom; Yukoh Tada: 86 bottom, 90 bottom, 130 top, 140, 161; Times Newspapers Ltd.: 24–5; Lise Torok: 128–9, 143, 147 top; J.R. Webber: 137.

Records and Principal Results

The BOC Challenge: Overall positions on elapsed times

Times given in days, hours, minutes and seconds

Position	Yacht/Skipper	Elapsed time, legs 1, 2, 3 & 4				Total elapsed time			
Class 1 yachts									
1	**Crédit Agricole**	47d	00h	01m	02s	159d	02h	26m	01s
	Philippe Jeantot	35d	09h	14m	16s				
		47d	23h	59m	08s				
		28d	17h	11m	35s				
2	**Altech Voortrekker**	53d	15h	54m	54s	170d	16h	51m	21s
	Bertie Reed	37d	03h	50m	53s				
		50d	03h	26m	55s				
		29d	17h	38m	39s				
3	**Perseverance of**	56d	18h	51m	19s	192d	10h	06m	48s
	Medina	50d	05h	05m	18s				
	Richard Broadhead	50d	09h	26m	11s[1]				
		35d	00h	44m	00s				
4	**Leda Pier One**	62d	17h	14m	50s	202d	02h	18m	25s
	Neville Gosson	45d	21h	08m	24s				
		58d	11h	11m	11s[2]				
		35d	00h	44m	00s[3]				
	Gipsy Moth V	57d	05h	05m	32s				
	Desmond Hampton	2nd leg, wrecked on Gabo Island, 18 December 1982							
	Lady Pepperell	57d	21h	47m	10s				
	Tony Lush	2nd leg, pitchpoled and sank, 28 November 1982							
	Spirit of Pentax	58d	23h	30m	23s				
	Paul Rodgers	2nd leg, retired after knockdown, 18 November 1982							
	Gladiator	76d	20h	42m	00s				
	David White	2nd leg, retired with self-steering problems, 21 November 1982							
Class 2 yachts									
1	**Koden Okera V**	59d	2h	52m	00s	207d	13h	55m	45s
	Yukoh Tada	53d	02h	23m	12s				
		56d	19h	47m	24s				
		36d	20h	53m	09s				
2	**Mooneshine**	60d	21h	29m	51s	209d	01h	32m	49s
	Francis Stokes	52d	04h	54m	28s[4]				
		59d	16h	39m	45s				
		36d	06h	28m	45s				
3	**Nike III**	65d	16h	38m	50s	213d	16h	46m	28s
	Richard Konkolski	63d	06h	42m	18s				
		52d	06h	12m	00s[5]				
		32d	11h	13m	20s				
4	**Ratso II**	68d	17h	06m	14s	221d	11h	50m	58s
	Guy Bernardin	52d	23h	11m	35s				
		62d	07h	55m	05s				
		37d	11h	38m	04s				

(continued overleaf)

1 Allows for Race Committee deduction of 145 hours for rescuing Jacques de Roux.
2 Allows for Race Committee deduction of 21 hours for turning back to aid rescue of Jacques de Roux.
3 Allows for Race Committee deduction of 25 hours 18 minutes for turning back to rescue Richard Konkolski.
4 Allows for Race Committee deduction of 12 hours 30 minutes for rescuing Tony Lush.
5 Allows for Race Committee deduction of 168 hours for time spent in port after late completion of second leg.

Class 2 yachts (continued)

5	**Fantasy** Dany Byrne	65d	12h	24m	15s	228d	09h	58m	53s
		56d	22h	34m	23s				
		66d	06h	42m	35s				
		39d	16h	17m	40s				
6	**City of Dunedin** Richard McBride	73d	09h	50m	47s	264d	04h	49m	50s
		55d	10h	52m	47s				
		96d	14h	58m	05s				
		38d	17h	08m	11s				

	Skoiern III Jacques de Roux	55d	19h	38m	08s
		46d	01h	30m	08s

3rd leg, pitchpoled and sank, 11 February 1983

Datsun Skyline 1st leg, elapsed time not available
Greg Coles On completion of leg retired with self-steering problems

Driftwood 1st leg, retired with engine and self-steering problems, 30
Thomas Lindholm August 1982

The BOC Challenge: Principal records set*

Skipper/Yacht	Record
Philippe Jeantot *Crédit Agricole* 17.07m (56ft)	1. Fastest solo circumnavigation of the world, with a time of 159 days, 2 hours, 6 minutes, beating by 10 days the previous best time, set in 1974 by the late Alain Colas in *Manureva* (formerly *Pen Duick IV*), a trimaran of 21.28m (69ft 10in) 2. Longest 7-day run, of 1552 miles, set on the third leg, between Sydney and Cape Horn, achieved from noon 8 February to noon 15 February 1983 3. Longest noon-to-noon run by a single-handed monohull during a circumnavigation, being 240 miles, achieved on 9–10 February 1983, on the third leg, between Sydney and Cape Horn
Richard Konkolski *Nike III* 13.41m (44ft)	1. Longest 24-hour run for a single-handed monohull during a circumnavigation, being 247 miles, set midnight to midnight on 26 February 1983, on the third leg, between Sydney and Cape Horn 2. Longest 7-day run during a circumnavigation by a small monohull, under 15.50m (50ft 10in) LOA, being, 1403 miles, from noon 20 April to noon 27 April 1983
Bertie Reed *Altech Voortrekker* 14.93m (49ft)	1. Fastest circumnavigation of the world by a small monohull, under 15.50m (50ft 10in) LOA, with a time of 170 days, 16 hours, 51 minutes, beating the previous best time of 224 days, set in 1981–82 by David Scott-Cowper in *Outward Bound*

* *Researched and compiled by D.H. Clarke*

The BOC Challenge: Additional Awards

Trophy	Awarded for	Recipient
BOC Best Log Award	Best navigational log for the entire voyage	**Neville Gosson**
BOC Overall Communications Award	Outstanding contribution in coordinating all communications throughout the race	**Rob Koziomkowski**
BOC Seamanship Awards	Outstanding seamanship, exemplified by the saving of two lives during the course of the race	**Richard Broadhead** **Francis Stokes**
Konkolski Bell	Best performance based on waterline length of boat	**Bertie Reed**

Index

Numbers in italics refer to
illustrations